done in a day
GARDEN projects

done in a day
GARDEN
projects

STEWART WALTON

MARSHALL PUBLISHING • LONDON

A Marshall Edition
Conceived, edited and designed by
Marshall Editions Ltd
The Orangery
161 New Bond Street
London W1Y 9PA

First published in the UK in 1998 by Marshall Publishing Ltd

ISBN 1-84028-194-4 (HB)
1-84028-121-9 (PB)

9 8 7 6 5 4 3 2 1

Project Editor Esther Labi
Designer Bridgewater Books
Managing Editor Clare Currie
Editorial Coordinator Rebecca Clunes
Art Director Sean Keogh
DTP Editor Lesley Gilbert
Production James Bann

Originated in Singapore by Master Image
Printed and bound in Italy

CONTENTS

INTRODUCTION

Does your garden consist solely of an expanse of grass and a few paving stones or shrubs? Perhaps you'd like to liven up your garden, patio or roof terrace but don't know where to start? Within these pages you'll find twelve exciting, inspirational garden features that will help you turn your back garden into a vibrant outdoor living area.

If you are planning a garden from scratch, focus on one or more of the garden projects, and design your garden around it; several projects would easily work together in one garden, depending on its size. If your garden is already established, you can adapt one of the projects to suit your own requirements. You may find it easier to reach for a pencil to sketch out your design before you reach for your tools. Watch the garden at different times of the day – what is the hottest part of the garden? Will any areas get winter sun? It is also worth investing in a soil tester and making a list of plants that are suitable for your soil type. Once you have decided what plants are going in your garden, you have to work out how to best display them.

There are projects that will appeal to the do-it-yourself novice and expert alike. If you are not very confident with wood-working techniques, try the **water feature**, a simple pond that involves very simple but effective tiling. If you don't want to try your hand at tiling, look at the homemade hammock – there's no sewing involved at all. Imagine lying next to your water feature, in your hammock – a picture of tranquility! If you've never tried bricklaying before, why not follow the easy steps and build a **brick barbecue** or a **raised herb bed**. Let all the family join in – you can use the herbs in marinades for the food for the barbecue, which the family are sure to enjoy.

Kids love to get involved in the garden, whether it's making mud pies in the boat-shaped **seaside sandbox** or growing seedlings and watching them bloom in **a perfect window box**. The **picnic table and seats** is another project that they can get involved in making – they'll love helping you paint it in bright colours.

If you enjoy watching wildlife, particularly birds, encourage them to feed in your garden by building the **rotund bird feeder**, which can be placed on a plinth or hung from a tree. Make or buy ready-made birdseed cakes or place a few scraps of bread in the bird feeder to attract birds all year round. In the spring, you may even be lucky enough to get a nesting pair of birds in the **tree-top birdhouse**. You can also grow certain shrubs and flowers that encourage butterflies and bees to come into your garden.

For a more structured garden, look at the projects that will help you add an architectural element to the landscape. Building a **garden obelisk**, for example, or maybe two obelisks joined by a shelf, will add geometry to your garden. To add interest at a different level, place a **picket-fence planter** next to it – to add some colour, make it with solid sides and paint it. If you already have different levels in your garden, link the levels with a stepped paved path. You can put your own personal stamp on your handiwork by adding pebbles or sweet-smelling thyme between the paving slabs.

A garden is more than just a collection of trees, shrubs and flowers. It can also be a nature reserve for wildlife or a tranquil haven from the daily stresses of modern living. What ever kind of garden you're hoping to create, these twelve garden projects will help you achieve it.

7

A NOTE ABOUT PLANTS:

The garden projects you choose to make will only look as good as the plants they're with, so make sure you take care of your garden. If you don't know much about plants, invest in a large plant encyclopedia; these list hundreds of plants and the conditions they grow best in, so do some research before you buy – dead plants can be costly. Along with water and food, a little care will turn your planting scheme into the garden of your dreams.

A NOTE ABOUT MEASUREMENTS:

The measurements and quantites given for each project are adaptable for different sizes and areas. Wherever possible, information is given to allow you to calculate how much material you need to customise the project. When working with tiles, make sure you allow for breakages and buy slightly more than you need. Measurements are given in imperial and metric, but only follow one set of measurements – do not interchange them.

Now that you are ready to attempt your first project, keep the following safety procedures in mind at all times:

❖ Several of the projects suggest protective clothing for certain activities and remember, accidents do happen so it is advisable to wear them;

❖ Always keep powertools unplugged while they are not in use;

❖ If you are working outdoors make sure that any powertool cables are kept clear of water;

❖ When working with a scalpel or utility knife, keep your steadying hand *well away* and *behind* your cutting hand;

❖ Wear goggles when breaking mirror tiles for the water feature (Project 5);

❖ Only cut MDF (Medium Density Fibreboard) in a well-ventilated area and wear the correct type of breathing mask.

HOW THIS BOOK WORKS

A brief introduction and description of each project

Tools needed for each project are illustrated

Exploded diagrams show how all the elements fit together

Step-by-step photographs provide a visual reference to accompany the text

Some boxes are "Professional Tip" boxes, which offer expert guidance on achieving the best results

Descriptive text accompanies each photograph, to ensure you know exactly what you are doing

Information boxes provide useful tips on products and procedures, providing alternative options and finishes

Close-up photographs of the finished projects show the end result

A variation of each project provides an interesting alternative

Variations are also illustrated in detail

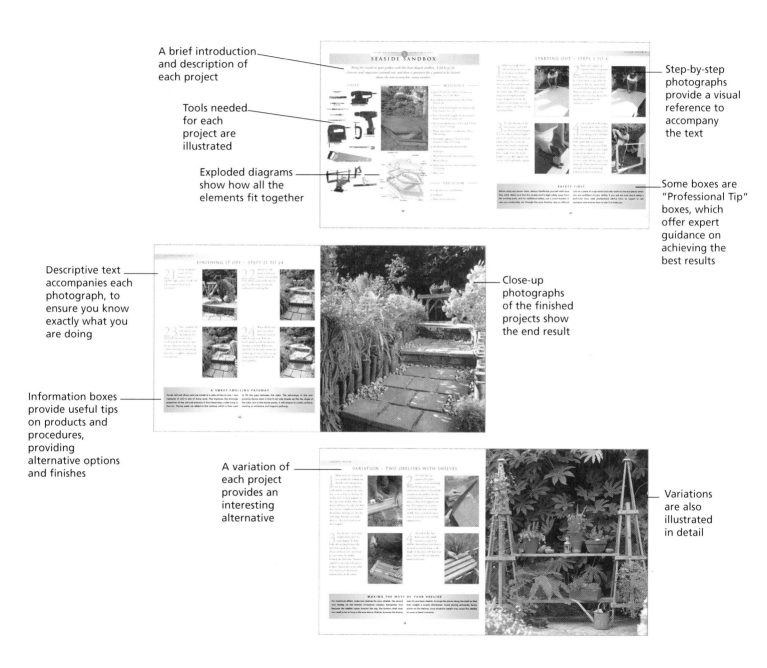

GARDEN OBELISK

Add a touch of style to your garden with this wooden obelisk. One can stand alone as a frame for climbing plants or runner beans. Or make two with shelves running between them for an unusual and attractive way of displaying pot plants.

TOOLS

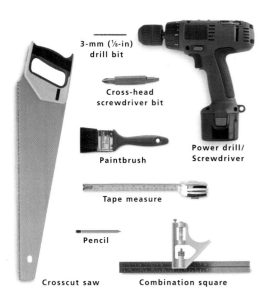

3-mm (⅛-in) drill bit

Cross-head screwdriver bit

Paintbrush

Power drill/ Screwdriver

Tape measure

Pencil

Crosscut saw

Combination square

MATERIALS

❖ Ten 1.8-m (6-ft) lengths 3.75-by 2cm (1½- by ¾-in) treated sawn wood

❖ No. 6 non-corrosive cross-head screws, 3cm (1¼ in), 3.75cm (1½ in) and 5cm (2 in) long

❖ Fence post cap

❖ Wood preservative

VARIATION

To make a second obelisk:

❖ Ten 1.8m (6-ft) lengths 3.75-x 2cm (1½- x ¾-in) treated sawn wood

❖ No. 6 non-corrosive cross-head screws, 3cm (1¼ in), 3.75cm (1½ in) and 5cm (2 in) long

❖ Fence post cap

❖ Wood preservative

For each shelf:

❖ Five 1.8-m (6-ft) lengths, 2.5 x 3.75cm (1 x 1½ in) treated sawn wood

❖ No. 8 non-corrosive cross-head screws

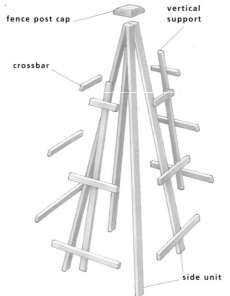

fence post cap

vertical support

crossbar

side unit

NOTE

The wood for this project can be bought from garden centres already treated with weatherproofer. If it is not treated, remember to weatherproof and, if you wish, stain it before you start work. The wood is sold in packs or individual lengths.

STARTING OUT ~ STEPS 1 TO 4

1 The obelisk is made up of two side units in the shape of an inverted V, linked together with crossbars. To make each side unit, take two 1.8-m (6-ft) lengths of wood and lay one on the ground, placing the other directly on top of it. Then, slide the lengths 45cm (18 in) apart at one end (this will be the foot). Make sure that the top end remains aligned, with one corner of the upper length directly over a corner of the lower length.

2 The top needs to mitred for a neat fit. To do this, hold the two pieces firmly in position at the top end, making sure that the corners remain aligned and that the foot ends remain 45cm (18 in) apart. Then, draw a pencil line across the lower length of wood, using the top piece as a guide. Repeat Steps 1 and 2 to mark the mitre for the other side unit.

3 Brace each side unit with three crossbars. Measuring from the bottom of one of the lengths of wood, mark the positions of the crossbars at 20, 70 and 118cm (8, 27¾ and 47¼ in). Use a combination square to draw a line at each of the three marks at right angles to the edge of the wood.

4 Use the marked-up length of wood as a guide to mark the position of the crossbars on the other three lengths of wood. Lay the wood on the ground, so that their ends align. Using your combination square or the edge of a crosscut saw, extend the three pencil lines onto the other three pieces of timber (see below).

PROFESSIONAL TIP

Most crosscut saws today have a square marked where the handle meets the straight edge of the blade. If your combination square is not long enough to reach over four pieces of wood, use the square on the saw. Butt the handle up to the edge of the wood, lining up the straight edge of the saw with the line on the first piece of wood. Then, continue this line over the other pieces of wood with your pencil, using the straight edge of the saw as a guide.

PUTTING IT TOGETHER - STEPS 5 TO 8

5 To cut the mitres you marked in Step 2, place the marked wood on a workbench. Using a crosscut saw, cut along the line. When sawing along a pencil line, always position your saw on the waste-wood side of the line. Saw steadily to achieve an even cut. Then cut the mitre for the other side unit.

6 To screw the top of the side units together, you need to drill pilot holes first. From the pointed top of the mitred piece, measure 7.5cm (3 in) and 12.5cm (5 in) down and mark these positions in the centre of the wood. Drill a hole at each point using the 3-mm (⅛-in) drill bit. Do the same to the mitred length of the other side unit.

7 Hold one mitred and one uncut length of wood together, making sure that the top is flat. Place a 3.75-cm (1½-in) screw in the top pilot hole and screw together, holding the two lengths of wood firmly in position. Then, place a 5-cm (2-in) screw in the lower pilot hole and screw into place. Repeat for the other side unit.

8 To measure the crossbars, lay one side unit on the ground. Position a 1.8-m (6-ft) length of wood so that its bottom edge is level with the guidelines drawn in Step 4. Mark the outside edges of the side unit on the length of wood in pencil. Move the wood up and along so that the bottom edge aligns with the next guidelines and mark the second crossbar. Then repeat for the third crossbar.

TREATING WOOD

It is essential to protect all the cut ends of the wood with wood preservative. Untreated wood will be affected by moisture, which will cause the wood to rot away, and will also be vulnerable to wood-eating insects. There are a variety of wood preservatives that have colour added to them to make a wood stain. These can look attractive because the grain of the wood still shows through. As the plants grow, they will obscure the obelisk, but you will still see glimpses of colour amid the foliage.

PUTTING IT TOGETHER – STEPS 9 TO 12

9 Place the wood on a workbench and cut along the marked guides. Measure and cut three more crossbars for the second side unit. You should now have two sets of crossbars, each set with three lengths.

10 The side units are linked by two more sets of crossbars. Each must be 3.75cm (1½ in) (two widths) longer than the crossbars already cut, to allow for the thickness of the uprights. To cut these, place one crossbar on another length of wood. At either end, place an offcut of wood on its edge and mark this position. Repeat for the other two lengths of crossbar and cut out two sets of crossbars.

11 You should now have four sets of crossbars, two *shorter* sets for the side units and two *longer* sets to link them. Avoid confusion by keeping the sets separated. To attach the shorter crossbars to the side units, drill a pilot hole 2cm (¾ in) from each end of the shorter crossbars. Position them using the guides drawn earlier and attach each one with 3-cm (1¼-in) screws.

12 The vertical length (see diagram on page 10) in the centre of each side unit provides extra support for climbing plants. Cut four 1.2-m (4-ft) lengths of wood. Turn the side units over, with the crossbars face down. Position a vertical in the centre of each side unit. The vertical should stand proud of the top and bottom crossbar by about 9cm (3½ in). Screw into place at each crossbar. Repeat for the other side unit.

TAKE CARE

When working on these projects, it is important that you are comfortable and can move around your work area freely and without having to climb over clutter. Make sure the area is tidy and that you have enough room to lay the wood flat. When sawing wood, position and hold it firmly at a comfortable height on a stable object such as a box, stool, workbench or a sawhorse. If you are working outside, make sure that you clear away any garden debris that could trip you as you work.

FINISHING IT OFF - STEPS 13 TO 16

13 Now join the two side units together. On the front of *one* of the side units, drill a pilot hole 2.5cm (1 in) down from the top. Stand the units up against each other, so that they are facing, their tops are level and the crossbars are on the outside. Holding the structures together firmly, secure them with a 3.75-cm (1½-in) screw in the pilot hole.

14 Drill pilot holes 1cm (⅜in) from each end of the *longer* (linking) crossbars. Attach only the bottom and middle crossbars to link the two sides, making sure that each end aligns with the crossbars already attached. Screw them into place using 3-cm (1¼-in) screws.

15 To add the last two vertical supports, drill a pilot hole 9cm (3½ in) from each end of the supports. Join a vertical to the centre of a top crossbar with a 3-cm (1¼-in) screw. Do the same for other the vertical support. Lay the obelisk with the longer crossbars face down on the ground, and fix the vertical support to the other two crossbars. Turn the obelisk around and attach the last vertical support in the same way.

16 As a finishing touch, add a fence post cap to the top of the obelisk. (If the top is not level and square, lay the obelisk on its side and saw off the top.) Drill a pilot hole in the middle of the post cap. Position the post cap on the top of the obelisk and screw it into position with a 3.75-cm (1½-in) screw. Finally, paint all the cut ends with wood preservative.

PLANNING YOUR PLANTS

An obelisk allows you to introduce an element of architecture into your garden, so spend some time choosing the best spot. It needs to be in an area where its geometric shape complements the organic shape of the surrounding plants. Remember to check the maximum height of any plants you plan to grow through your obelisk, to make sure that they will not grow too big for the structure. Also, make sure that plants grow evenly around the structure, so that their weight will not cause it to overbalance.

VARIATION – TWO OBELISKS WITH SHELVES

1 Make more of a feature for your garden by making two obelisks and linking them with one or two slatted shelves. Each obelisk is made in the same way as far as Step 14. In Step 15, do not add a vertical support to the side of the obelisk where the shelves will rest. To make the shelf slats, lay four lengths of wood on the ground, making sure that the ends align. Measure and mark them at 1.2m (4 ft) and cut off these lengths.

2 The shelf slats are supported by three supports, each measuring 20.5cm (8¼ in), which is the inside measurement of the middle crossbar on the obelisk. On the remaining wood, measure, mark and cut three shelf supports this size. The supports sit at either end of the shelf and across the middle. For a neat finish, cut a mitre at each end of the middle support piece.

3 Lay the four 1.2-m (4-ft) lengths down with the ends aligned. To help make the spacing between the shelf slats equal, place three offcuts of the 2-cm (¾-in) wood left over from the obelisk, between the shelf slats. Position a support at one end and screw it in place. Repeat this at the other end, then attach the mitred support piece in the centre.

4 The end of the shelf hooks over the middle crossbar of each of the obelisks. You will find that there is no need to screw it down, as the weight of the plants will hold it in place. Paint all the cut ends with wood preservative.

MAKING THE MOST OF YOUR OBELISK

For maximum effect, make two shelves for your obelisk, the second one resting on the bottom horizontal crossbar. Remember that because the obelisk tapers toward the top, the bottom shelf does not need to be as long as the one above. Shelves increase the display area of your basic obelisk. Arrange the plants along the shelf so that their weight is evenly distributed. Avoid placing extremely heavy plants on the shelves, since excessive weight may cause the obelisk to warp or bend unevenly.

A PERFECT WINDOW BOX

A window box overflowing with foliage and flowers adds a dramatic splash of colour to even the smallest space. This one is intended to hold plants that have not been removed from their pots, allowing you to change your arrangement at will.

TOOLS

3-mm (¹⁄₈-in) drill bit

Filler knife

Paintbrush

Cordless drill/
Screwdriver

Jigsaw

Wire cutters

Pencil

Crosscut saw

Tape measure

Combination square

Hammer

MATERIALS

❖ One 2.4-m (8-ft) length, or two 1.2-m (4-ft) lengths 15- by 2.5-cm (6- by 1-in) treated sawn wood

❖ Sandpaper

❖ No. 6 non-corrosive cross-head screws, 6cm (2½-in) long

❖ One 1.2-m (4-ft) length 3.75- by 2.5-cm (1½- by 1-in) treated sawn wood

❖ One 1.5-m (5-ft) length 3.75- by 2-cm (1½- by ¾-in) treated sawn wood

❖ Panel pins, 16mm (⅝ in) long

❖ Exterior wood filler

❖ Wood stain or preservative

❖ Roofing slate tiles

❖ Quarter-round moulding, 6mm (¼ in) wide

❖ About four potted plants

VARIATION

❖ Quarter-round moulding, 6mm (¼ in) wide

❖ Panel pins, 16mm (⅝ in) long

❖ One 1.2-m (4-ft) length 3.75- by 2-cm (1½- by ¾-in) treated sawn wood

❖ Wire mesh, 1.25-cm (½-in) gauge

❖ Screws

❖ Five ceramic tiles, 15 by 15cm (6 by 6 in)

❖ Sandpaper

❖ Cedar trellis

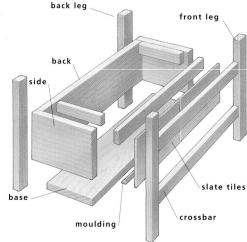

back leg

front leg

back

side

base

moulding

slate tiles

crossbar

NOTE

If you do not have a suitable windowsill on which to position your window box, attach an old shelf unit to the wall under a window. Alternatively, support the box on a row of bricks to aid drainage and place the box at the base of an outside wall.

STARTING OUT – STEPS 1 TO 4

1 Mark out the basic box: on the length of 15-cm (6-in) wide wood, measure and mark the following lengths: 79cm (31½ in) for the base, 74cm (29½ in) for the back, and two lengths of 21.5cm (8½ in) for each side. Use a combination square to help you draw straight lines across the wood at each of these points.

2 Cut each of the lengths of wood along the lines you have drawn. When you have cut the four pieces, lightly sand the cut ends to remove any splinters. Do not sand the ends too smoothly because they will not be consistent with the overall rough texture of the wood.

3 On one of the side pieces draw a line 2.5cm (1 in) in from one of the short sides. Within this width, drill a pilot hole in each corner. Do the same for the other side piece. Attach the side pieces to the back piece with a screw in each pilot hole.

4 Drill pilot holes into each corner of the base, about 1.25cm (½ in) in from the edges. Place the base on top of the back and sides so that the gap (for drainage) is towards the back of the window box. Hold the base firmly and secure it into the side pieces through the pilot holes, using the 6-cm (2½-in) screws.

PROFESSIONAL TIP

If you make absolutely sure that all the box sides are exactly equal in height and that right angles are accurate, then the box will be easy to assemble. Check the right angles using a combination square. Making square cuts with a hand saw will be easier if you clamp a length of scrap wood along the cutting line to guide the blade. Sand raw edges only lightly to prevent rounding of the angles for a more secure bond, apply a thin layer of wood glue to the pieces before screwing them together.

PUTTING IT TOGETHER – STEPS 5 TO 8

5 On the piece of 3.75- by 2.5-cm (1½- by 1-in) wood, measure and mark two 29.5-cm (11½-in) lengths for the back legs and two 30-cm (12-in) lengths for the front legs (see below). Cut these lengths out, then lightly sand the cut ends of each leg.

6 The front of the window box is made from two crossbars. Measure and mark two lengths of 71.5cm (28½ in) on the 3.75- by 2-cm (1½- by ¾-in) wood and cut these out. Lightly sand the cut ends to remove any splinters.

7 To make the front panel, mark a point 4.5cm (1¾ in) and 21cm (8½ in) from one end on the narrow side of each front leg. Draw a straight line across the wood at these points. On the wider side of each leg, mark a point 6cm (2½ in) and 23cm (9¼ in) from the same end, and drill pilot holes at these points. Screw the crossbars to the legs, aligning the bottom edge of each crossbar with one of the lines drawn on the narrow side of the legs.

8 On the narrow side of the back legs, mark a line 7.5cm (3 in) and 22.5cm (9 in) from one end. Mark and drill two evenly spaced pilot holes in between these two lines, but on the wider face of each leg. Align the pencil marks with the top and bottom of the back of the box, and screw the legs in place. Turn the box over and place the front panel you made in Step 7 on top. Align the pencil marks and secure in place.

PROFESSIONAL TIP

Before you cut the legs, consider the way your windowsill lies. Windowsills usually slope away from the window to allow rainwater to drain off. By making the front legs slightly longer than the back legs, the window box is set at an angle opposite to that of the sill. This allows the base of the box to remain level and ensures that none of the plants become waterlogged – a possibility if the window box tilts at an angle. If your windowsill is completely level, cut all the legs the same length.

PUTTING IT TOGETHER ~ STEPS 9 TO 12

9 Make an interior frame for the front panel of the window box to keep the slate tiles in place. Mark the length of the inside front of the box on the quarter-round moulding by placing one end of it in one corner of the box, then marking where to cut it at the other end.

10 The moulding forms the bottom of the interior frame, but there must be room for a slate tile between the moulding and the crossbar at the front. On the inside of the front panel, hold a tile against the crossbars, then push the moulding against the bottom of the tile. Secure the moulding on the bottom crossbar with panel pins.

11 Now make the top of the interior frame. Measure and mark a length of 3.75- by 2-cm (1½- by ¾-in) wood against the inside top of the box, as you did with the moulding. Cut the wood to size. Hold a tile in place, as before, and secure the wood to the inside of window box with 3.75-cm (1½-in) screws.

12 Measure and cut two side pieces from the length of 3.75- by 2-cm (1½- by ¾-in) wood. You can use a tape measure or you can just mark the length as you did with the moulding in Step 9. Repeat for the other side. Drill a pilot hole into the centre of each side piece and position them on the inside, level with the front of the interior frame and the top of the window box. Fix them into place with 3.75-cm (1½-in) screws.

STAINS AND PRESERVATIVES

Wood stains soak into the wood, allowing the character and grain of the wood to show through. Because the stain used here is water-based, the brushes can easily cleaned with water. Some stains have preservatives added to them, which further protects the wood against the elements. Whether you decide to stain your window box or just treat it with wood preservative, make sure that the product you choose does not contain any hazardous chemicals that could harm the plants. Always check the manufacturer's instructions.

FINISHING IT OFF – STEPS 13 TO 16

13 Your window box is almost ready for painting. To give an even surface, fill the visible screw holes with exterior wood filler. Allow the filler to dry (see manufacturer's instructions for drying time).

14 Once the filler is dry, lightly sand over the filled area. You do not need to sand until the filler is completely smooth, just enough so that its texture matches the surrounding wood.

15 Before you paint the window box, protect your work surface with some newspaper and stand the box on top. Using a brush, paint the bottom of the box first, then turn it over and paint the inside. Paint the outside, the front, back and sides last.

16 Measure and mark two pieces, 15 by 36.5cm (6 by 14½ in), on the slate. Use chalk to mark this, rather than pencil, as it will show up better. Wearing goggles, hold the slate firmly on the edge of a table or workbench and cut along the lines with a jigsaw. Place the cut slate into the panel at the front of the window box.

CHANGING THE LOOK OF YOUR WINDOW BOX

Ceramic tiles come in a variety of colours, designs and finishes – and the beauty of this window box is that you can ring the changes whenever you wish. Simply slot your chosen tiles into the interior frame in the front panel of the window box. If you decide from the start to use tiles rather than roof slate-tiles, make the interior frame an appropriate size to accommodate them. You can vary the choice of tiles to suit the season or to complement the plants you have chosen for your window box.

VARIATIONS – ALTERNATIVE FRONT PANELS

1 A piece of cedar trelliswork slotted into the interior frame makes an alternative front panel for the window box. Expand the trelliswork and lay it down so that it forms perfect diamond shapes. It may be helpful to clamp a length of wood to the trellis to hold it rigid as you cut it. Measure the inside of the front panel and transfer the measurement to the front of the trellis to fit.

2 Use a long straight edge, such as a length of wood, to mark the trellis. Use a jigsaw to cut along these lines, as this will be easier than using a crosscut saw (see below). Lightly sand the cut ends, then stain the trelliswork if you wish. Saturate the cut ends with wood preservative to prevent water penetration. When the stain is dry, position the trelliswork in the frame at the front of the box.

3 Mesh can also be used as a front panel. Measure the length and height of the inside of the frame and transfer these measurements to the mesh – the mesh needs to overlap the inside of the frame. Cut the mesh with wire cutters. With the box face down, place the mesh on the inside. Hold it in place with panel pins: hammer in the pin halfway, then hit it on the side so that it bends over.

4 Cutting mitres at the top of the legs makes an attractive finish. Mark the midpoint at the top of each side of the legs. Then, on the edge of each leg, mark a point 3.75cm (1½ in) down from the top. Join these points to the midpoint at the top. Lay the box on its side and saw along these diagonal lines to cut the mitres. Once cut, lightly sand the ends.

PROFESSIONAL TIP

Cedar trelliswork needs to be cut with care to prevent it from falling apart. When measuring and marking the lines to cut make sure they are close to the fixing points on the trelliswork. Even if the trelliswork does collapse, you can fix it into the frame on the window box, which will then support it. To repair a broken trellis, gently hammer in small panel pins with a pin hammer. The pins will not be noticed if you use a nail punch to push them into the wood. You can then cover them with exterior wood filler.

ROTUND BIRD FEEDER

Encourage birds to visit your garden by providing them with somewhere to rest and feed in safety. This simple feeder with its attractive overlapping slatted roof can either be suspended from the branch of a tree or stand on top of a plinth.

TOOLS

Nail punch

Pencil

Paintbrush

Utility knife

Power drill/
Screwdriver

Jigsaw

Tape measure

Hammer

Combination square

MATERIALS

❖ Pine shelf, 60 by 120cm (2 by 4 ft), 2cm (¾ in) thick

❖ Piece of scrap wood, at least 40 cm (16 in) long

❖ Treated sawn wood, 5 by 5cm (2 by 2 in), 60cm (2ft) long

❖ Cedar fencing, 1.2m (4 ft), 1cm (⅜ in) thick

❖ Plywood, 45 by 60cm (18 by 24 in), 3mm (⅛ in) thick

❖ Small round object to use as a guide

❖ Wood adhesive

❖ Wood stain or varnish

❖ Panel pins, 2cm (¾ in) long

❖ No. 8 screws, 3.75cm (1½ in) and 5cm (2 in) long

❖ Cardboard (optional, see Step 9)

❖ Oval nails, 2cm (¾ in) long

❖ Drill bit, 3mm (⅛ in) in diameter

VARIATION

❖ Doweling, 1.25cm (½ in) in diameter, at least 25cm (10 in) long

❖ Drill bit 1.25cm (½ in) wide

❖ Wooden drawer knob

❖ Hook

❖ Chain

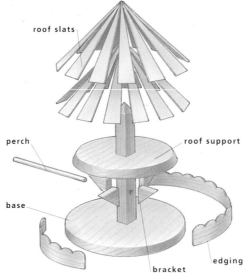

roof slats

perch

roof support

base

bracket

edging

NOTE

When positioning your bird feeder, make the safety of the birds your prime consideration. Do not stand it on top of any plinth that can be scaled by cats. Similarly, do not hang it in a tree that is frequented by cats or squirrels. Bird feeders are fun for children, who can make up their own birdseed cakes for birds to enjoy. But having tempted birds to your garden, be prepared to go on feeding them, for they will become dependent on the food you offer.

STARTING OUT – STEPS 1 TO 4

1 Start by drawing two circles on the pine shelf – one 37.5cm (15 in) in diameter, the other 40cm (16 in). To make a "compass" large enough, hammer a small nail through one end of the piece of scrap wood. Mark points 17.5cm (7½ in) and 20cm (8 in) from the nail and drill a hole, just big enough for a pencil. Make a small hole in the pine to rest the nail in, then draw the circles using the nail as the pivot.

2 Measure a 42.5-cm (17-in) length on the treated sawn wood. (This will be the post in the middle of your bird feeder.) Place the wood over the edge of a table or workbench and cut the length off.

3 Trace around the end of the post in the middle of each circle. To do this accurately, draw a line through the nail hole in the centre of each circle. Then draw another line at right angles to this line, also passing through the nail hole at the centre. Position the corners of the post on these lines and then draw around the post with a pencil.

4 Place the pine on a table or workbench and using your jigsaw, cut out the 40-cm (16-in) circle with a jigsaw. Then, adjust your jigsaw to a 45° angle and cut out the 37.5-cm (15-in) circle at this angle. The sloped edge will make it easier to attach the roof later.

PROFESSIONAL TIP

Sometimes you need to cut out an area in the middle of a piece of wood without cutting into it from the side (see Step 5). To do this, drill a short row of small holes (on the waste side of the guidelines on the wood) in such a way that the holes join together, to make an opening large enough for you to fit the blade of the jigsaw through. You may need to push a screwdriver or sharp object through the holes to join them together. Once you have inserted the jigsaw blade, you can cut along the guidelines.

PUTTING IT TOGETHER – STEPS 5 TO 8

5 Cut out the squares for the post in the centre of each circle (see the tip box on page 27). It is better if you undercut the first time as you can trim or sand it to fit in Step 8.

6 To make the point at the top end of the post, mark the midpoint on each of the top edges of the post. Using a combination square, draw a line at 45° from this mark to the long edges of the post on all sides. Cut these portions off and sand the rough edges to remove any splinters.

7 Using the wood left over from the cut circles, make four brackets (see below). Once you have cut these, sand the edges. Drill a pilot hole into each bracket through the width of the longest side. Measure 17cm (6¾ in) down from the top of the post. Use a combination square to draw a straight line around the post at this point. Set each bracket on this line and attach each one to the post with a 5-cm (2-in) screw.

8 Push the post through the hole in the larger circle to make the base. It should be a tight fit. Push the post through the smaller circle so it rests on the brackets. Secure this in place through the top of the circle with 3.75-cm (1½-in) screws. For extra security, hammer some nails through the base at an angle, so that they enter the post.

MAKING BRACKETS

The easiest brackets to make are right-angled triangles. Draw two perpendicular lines 5.5cm (2¼ in) long. Join them to make the third line of the triangle and cut the triangle out. When joining the brackets to the post, remember that if screws are put directly into wood there is a risk of splitting it. Drilling pilot holes prevents splitting and ensures accuracy. Use a drill bit one size smaller than the screw size and drill to at least half its depth. This will allow the screw threads to fix securely.

PUTTING IT TOGETHER – STEPS 9 TO 12

9 The roof is made up of two different-sized slats made from the plywood; and you need twelve of each. One set of slats measure 7.5 by 30cm (3 by 12 in) and the others measure 6 by 30cm (2½ by 12 in). Cut out all 24 pieces with a jigsaw. If necessary, make a cardboard template: you need to make two triangles 30cm (12 in) high, one with a 6-cm (2½-in) base, the other with a 7.5-cm (3-in) base.

10 Take all the 7-cm- (3-in-) wide slats and hold them together on their sides. Using a pencil or pen, measure 2.5cm (1 in) from the wide end. Using a combination square, draw a straight line at this point across all the edges. These marks will act as a guide so that you can align the slats when attaching them to the bird feeder. Do the same for the other slats.

11 Start assembling the roof by fixing four of the 7.5-cm (3-in) slats to the top of the post in the position of the four points of the compass. Hold each one in place with a panel pin at the top of each slat. Leave the bottom edge loose for the moment.

12 Now position two 7.5-cm (3-in) slats in between each of the four already in place. Nail these to the post at the top and trim the points with a utility knife if they overlap at the top. There should be a gap of about 3.75cm (1½ in) between each slat when all twelve of them are in place. When you are happy with their positions, secure them in place at the bottom with panel pins.

ATTACHING THE SLATS

This type of roof is built up in layers, with the top slats filling the gaps and slightly overlapping the ones below. Any wear and tear on the roof will come from the weather, not from the bird visitors, so the shape of the slats is very important, and you should aim for a snug fit. Panel pins are sufficient to secure the slats and they are small enough to tap in place without splitting the wood. To make it easier to fit all the tips of the slats, sand back the mitred edges at the top of the post.

FINISHING IT OFF – STEPS 13 TO 16

13 The slightly smaller slats form the overlaps on the roof. Fix these into place with a panel pin at the top and bottom. Trim the top of the slats with a utility knife for a neat finish.

14 Cut two lengths of cedar fencing, one 37.5cm (15 in) long, and the other 75cm (30 in) long. Draw two parallel lines along the length, one 4cm (1¼ in) from the bottom, the other 5cm (1¾ in) from the bottom. Using a round object as a guide, draw curves in between these parallel lines. Cut out the pattern with a jigsaw.

15 Using wood adhesive, glue the scalloped pieces into place around the edge of the base. Tack it securely into place with evenly spaced panel pins. Leave two gaps of about 5cm (2 in) between the scalloped pieces to allow rainwater to escape and to make cleaning the bird feeder easier.

16 Stain or varnish the bird feeder to protect it from the elements. The stain will improve with age and a winter outside will season the bird feeder and make it look even more attractive.

BENDING WOOD

When you have cut out the scalloped edge for the bird feeder, you may find it difficult to bend it into shape. Get someone to hold it in position while you glue and pin the edge around the base. If you experience difficulty when attaching it to the bird feeder, try soaking your scalloped edge in water for about one hour. This should make it more pliable since wood is easier to bend when wet. If you soak the wood, remember that you will have to wait until the wood has dried out a little before you paint it.

VARIATION – A HANGING FEEDER

1 You may like to add a perch to the bird feeder. Measure and cut a piece of doweling to a length of about 25cm (10 in). This will be a suitable size for most small birds.

2 Drill a hole in the post 1.25cm (½ in) in diameter and work the dowel through – it needs to be quite a snug fit so that the perch is secure. Make sure it is roughly even on each side, and then paint it with a wood stain or varnish.

3 To attach a hook, you need to fit the top of your bird feeder with a wooden drawer pull first. Cut the bottom off the wooden drawer knob – you will need to secure it in a vice to steady it as you cut. Then hollow it out slightly with a drill so that it will sit on the pointed top of the bird feeder. Using wood adhesive, glue the drawer knob into position and protect it with wood preservative or varnish.

4 Choose a hook that is long enough to go through the drawer knob and into the post. Screw the hook through the middle of the drawer knob. (Depending on the size of your hook, you may have to drill a pilot hole first.) Using a length of chain, hang your bird feeder from the desired location.

WEATHERPROOFING THE CROWN

Any sawn edges of the slats must be saturated with wood stain so that the preservative can sink right into it. The crown will be even more watertight if it is capped and we used part of a wooden drawer knob for ours. This had the advantage of also being strong enough to take a hanging hook. You could substitute a crown of zinc, copper or asphalt material cut to a decorative scallop. But whatever you choose, make sure that you seal all screw or pin holes with exterior wood glue, in order to prevent water from getting in.

PICKET-FENCE PLANTER

Lend an air of decorative distinction to your garden with this capacious planter. The sides can be in "picket-fence" style if you want a rustic effect. Alternatively, use featherboarding to make solid sides and paint it a sophisticated black.

TOOLS

3-mm (⅛-in) drill bit

2.5-cm (1-in) flat drill bit

Pencil

Combination square

Cordless drill/ Screwdriver

Cross-head screwdriver bit

Tape measure

Paintbrush

Nail punch

Hammer

Crosscut saw

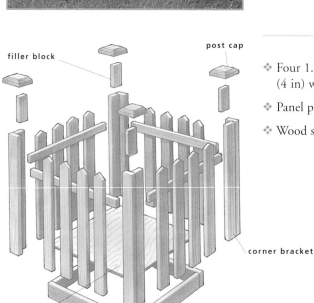

filler block

post cap

corner bracket

base

crossbar

MATERIALS

❖ Eight 1.8-m (6-ft) lengths treated sawn wood, 3.75 by 2cm (1½ by ¾ in)

❖ Piece of plywood, 42.5 by 42.5cm (17 by 17 in), 1.25cm (½ in) thick

❖ Oval brad nails, 3.75cm (1½ in) long

❖ Non-corrosive cross-head screws, 3cm (1¼ in) long

❖ Four fence post caps

❖ Wood preservative

❖ Planter, 30cm (12 in) in diameter

VARIATION

❖ Four 1.8-m (6-ft) lengths featheredge, 10cm (4 in) wide

❖ Panel pins, 2cm (¾ in) long

❖ Wood stain

NOTE

This planter makes a perfect companion to the garden obelisk (page 10). It provides a simple way to vary the height of the architectural elements in your garden.

STARTING OUT – STEPS 1 TO 4

1 Start by making the corners for the planter. The four corner brackets provide the main structural support and each corner is made from two 45-cm (18-in) pieces of wood. Measure 45cm (18 in) on one of the lengths of 3.75- by 2-cm (1½- by ¾-in) treated wood. Mark the position with a pencil, using a combination square to help you draw a straight line.

2 Saw off this length, remembering to position the saw on the waste side of the line. Use this 45-cm (18-in) length as a template for the remaining pieces; or measure each piece as you go, and cut out eight more 45-cm (18-in) lengths.

3 The corners of the planter are joined by crossbars at the top and bottom. You need eight crossbars in total – four at 44cm (17½ in) long and four at 39cm (15½ in) long. Measure and cut one 44-cm (17½-in) length and use this length as a template to cut the other three. Repeat the procedure to cut the four 39-cm (15½-in) crossbars.

4 Now assemble the corner brackets. Lay one 45-cm (18-in) length on its narrow face. Place another one on top, on its wide face, so that a right angle is formed between the two lengths to make a corner. Secure the pieces of wood together by hammering an oval brad nail about 3.75cm (1½ in) from each end and in the middle. Make the three other corner brackets in the same way.

WORKING SAFELY AND WELL

When sawing wood, make sure that you work at a height that is comfortable for you. If you do not have a workbench or saw horse, an adjustable stool, such as the one used here, can be altered to suit the individual and is ideal for sawing small lengths of wood. Make sure that you can support the wood as you cut it and that you do not need to stretch or stoop while working. Position the wood so that your cutting line overlaps the edge of your stool and use even strokes when sawing.

FINISHING IT OFF - STEPS 13 TO 16

13 Lay four of the pickets on the ground and place the planter on top of the pickets. Make sure that the points and ends of the pickets align. Using a piece of wood as a guide, space the pickets evenly between the corner brackets. Mark the position of the pickets on the crossbars, and then mark the position of pilot holes on both crossbars within the lines you have just drawn.

14 Drill pilot holes on the crossbars using the 3-mm (⅛-in) drill bit, then reposition the pickets underneath, using the marks you made as a guide. Again, make sure that the points and the ends of the pickets align. Attach the pickets to the crossbars with a screw in each pilot hole. Then turn the planter onto another side and repeat until the four sides are complete.

15 Place the base in the planter with the lines uppermost. You need to cut out drainage holes for excess water. Mark five holes, one in the centre and the others at four corners of a square around it, on the diagonal lines you drew in Step 10. Raise the planter on blocks of scrap lumber to keep the drill from hitting the ground. Cut the holes using the 2.5-cm (1-in) flat drill bit.

16 Before you add a fence post cap to each corner of the planter, cut a small piece of wood as a "filler" block in each corner, to help hold the caps securely. (Each filler block should be flush with the top of a corner, and sit on top of the crossbar.) Nail the filler block in place, then nail a fence post cap on top. Nail-punch the nail heads below the surface of the wood and paint all the cut ends and nails with wood preservative.

LOOKING AFTER YOUR PLANTS

Your hard work is done, and now you need to position your planter and add suitable potted plants. Remember to add drainage material at the bottom of the pot and then a soil mixture suitable to the type of plants you plan to grow. Slow-release plant-food granules keep container plants healthy and can be mixed into the soil before planting. Follow the manufacturer's instructions carefully, since overfeeding will burn the plant roots. Remember to water the plants regularly too, as potted plants do tend to dry out quickly.

VARIATION - A PLANTER WITH SOLID SIDES

1 Follow the instructions to make the planter up to and including Step 10. Add the filler blocks following the instructions in Step 16 (see page 38), attaching them to the top of each corner above the horizontal crossbar. Then nail a fence post cap over each corner.

2 To make one side, cut four 42.5-cm (17-in) lengths of featheredge. Lay the planter on its side and position a piece of featheredge so that its thin edge butts the top crossbar of the planter. Secure in place with panel pins on either side. Nail the next piece so that the thin edge overlaps the thick edge of the one already in place. Position and nail the other two pieces in the same way.

3 Turn the planter upside down and repeat the process on the opposite side with four more 42.5-cm (17-in) lengths. Then, cut eight 40-cm (16-in) lengths of featheredge for the other two sides. Attach these to the sides of the planter as before.

4 Taking care not to splash the surrounding area, paint the planter inside and out with a water-based wood stain. While you wait for the paint to dry, measure and add a base as in Step 15 (see page 38), remembering to drill drainage holes. Then position the planter in the garden and add a pot of your favourite plants.

PROFESSIONAL TIP

Use a water-based wood stain for this planter, as it is non-toxic to plants or animals and any spills or splashes can be removed quite easily with a damp cloth. As with any wooden structure, the look of this planter will improve with age.

After a season or two of exposure to the elements, the planter will have weathered and will take on a more rustic look. The type of pot you use inside this solid-sided planter is a matter of practicality rather than aesthetics, since it will not be visible.

WATER FEATURE

Water features make a welcome and attractive addition to any garden. The advantage of this one is that it can go anywhere, does not need a lot of space and requires no electricity or plumbing. It is also inexpensive and simple to make!

TOOLS

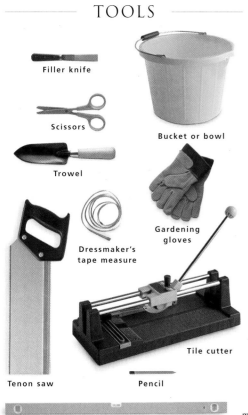

Filler knife

Scissors

Bucket or bowl

Trowel

Dressmaker's tape measure

Gardening gloves

Tile cutter

Tenon saw

Pencil

Spirit level

MATERIALS

❖ Glazed plant pot, the one used here is 50cm (20 in) high and 65cm (25 in) in diameter

❖ Two-part epoxy putty

❖ Piece of scrap wood, at least 15cm (6 in) long

❖ Ready-mixed quick-drying waterproof cement and a stick for stirring

❖ Mirror tiles (see Step 1 to calculate number)

❖ Ceramic strip tiles, (see Step 1 to calculate number)

❖ All-purpose waterproof wall tile adhesive and grout

❖ Dwarf lily, such as *Nymphaea pygmaea* 'Alba', double marsh marigold and iris

❖ Lily basket

❖ Piece of hessian sheet, at least 45 by 45cm (18 by 18 in)

❖ Aquatic compost

❖ Gravel

❖ Several bricks (see Step 16)

❖ Stick with rounded end

❖ Sponge

❖ Sandpaper

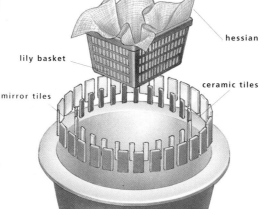

hessian

lily basket

ceramic tiles

mirror tiles

glazed pot

NOTES

Choose a sunny spot in your garden for this feature, waterlilies do not like shade.

Mirror tiles alternating with blue ceramic strip tiles maximize the reflection from the water. Remember to buy a few extra mirror tiles in case they break when you are cutting them.

Always wear gloves when using cement, especially if you have sensitive skin,

PUTTING IT TOGETHER - STEPS 1 TO 4

1 To work out how many tiles you need, measure the inside circumference of the pot with a dressmaker's tape measure. The width of one ceramic strip tile and one mirror tile together is 5cm (2 in) so divide the circumference by 5cm (2 in) to work out how many mirror and strip tiles you will need. (You can cut the mirror tiles to a different width in Step 6, but you will have to work out how many you need.)

2 Knead together the two-part epoxy putty following the manufacturer's instructions. Once it is a uniform colour, push it firmly into the drainage holes at the bottom of the pot, making sure that they are filled completely. This will stop the water from leaking out when the pot is full. Leave the putty to dry.

3 To create a level surface for the tiles, you will need to fill the slight depression under the rim on the inside of the pot with cement. To make a level for the cement, cut the scrap piece of wood to the same length as the tiles, 15cm (6 in), using a tenon saw.

4 Wearing a pair of gloves, pour the cement into a bowl. Make a well in the middle, then slowly add some water. Use a stick to mix the cement to a thick consistency, adding more water or cement as necessary. If you have not mixed enough to coat the rim of the pot, don't worry – just mix some more to the same consistency as you go.

PROFESSIONAL TIP

When mixing cement, remember that it sets very quickly, so always mix small quantities. Take care not to add too much water or the cement will be sloppy and difficult to work with. As a general rule, the cement is the right consistency when a stick or twig will stand vertically in the mix. If your cement is too dry, it will crumble and won't hold properly. In this case, simply add more water, a little at a time, until the cement is the required consistency.

PUTTING IT TOGETHER – STEPS 5 TO 8

5 Using a filler knife, apply a coat of cement to the inside of the pot, extending down 15cm (6 in). Take the cut piece of wood and hold it at right angles to, and level with, the top of the pot (use a spirit level to help you). Press down firmly, then slowly bring the wood around the pot towards you, pushing any excess cement away. Fill in any gaps with cement, then go over them again with the wood.

6 Now prepare the mirror tiles. Set the gauge on the tile cutter to a width of 3.75cm (1½ in). Butt the mirror tile up against the gauge, and bring the handle towards you to score the surface of the tile. Remember, always wear gloves when cutting mirror tiles.

7 Now bring the scored mirror tile up to the cutter, and position it under the cutting bars. Make sure that you hold the tile straight on the horizontal and bring the handle down in one swift movement. The required width will snap off. You should now have a mirror tile measuring 3.75 by 15cm (1½ by 6 in). Repeat for the other mirror tiles.

8 Sand all the edges of the mirror tiles to prevent harming people, pets or wildlife. To do this safely, lay a sheet of sandpaper on a flat surface and hold the mirror tile face down, at 45° to the sandpaper. Rub the tile back and forth several times to blunt the edges.

GEOMETRIC TILING

If you are feeling adventurous, or are an experienced tiler, you may like to try creating a more intricate design with the tiles. You can buy mosaic tiles either loose or in sheets, which can be cut to size. They come in a range of colours and can be mixed with the mirror tiles if you wish. You need to make a paper pattern the same size as the inside of the pot and lay out the pieces on it. Allow enough space between the tiles for the cement and transfer the pattern onto the pot, working a small section at a time.

PUTTING IT TOGETHER - STEPS 9 TO 12

9 When the cement is dry (about two hours), apply an even coat of tile adhesive using the applicator supplied with the adhesive. The glue should cover the surface of the cement strip all the way around the inside of the pot. The notches in the applicator create a good key for the tiles, enhancing the bond.

10 Start fixing the tiles in place. You will need to use a spirit level to make sure that the tiles remain vertical. Start with a mirror tile and hold it in place with the spirit level on top. Adjust the position of the tile as necessary so that it is vertical before you push it firmly into place.

11 Alternate ceramic and mirror tiles, keeping them at right angles to the top of the pot. As you push the tiles into place, excess adhesive will squeeze out of the gaps between them. Wipe this away with a sponge or cloth before it dries. Remember to keep checking that the tiles are vertical, using the spirit level to help you.

12 When the adhesive is dry (it should take about two hours), grout the tiles to prevent water from getting behind them. Use the straight edge of the adhesive applicator to apply the grout over the joins and in a layer around the top and bottom of the tiles. Run a stick in between the gaps of the tiles to compact the grout. Wipe off any excess grout on the tiles with a wet sponge before it dries.

PROFESSIONAL TIP

When choosing the tile adhesive, make sure that you select a waterproof variety, as it will be under water when it is dry. You may find that you need to choose between a thin-bed and a thick-bed adhesive. Select a thin-bed adhesive as it is simpler to use and can easily be spread to the required thickness – about 3mm (⅛ in). Thick-bed adhesive is more difficult to work with and is not recommended for beginners. It is used on uneven surfaces and requires considerable tiling skill.

FINISHING IT OFF – STEPS 13 TO 16

13 While you are waiting for the grout to dry, prepare the lily for planting. Line the lily basket with hessian, allowing the excess to hang over the sides. The hessian allows the plant's roots to grow through it and holds the compost in place. With a trowel, fill the basket with about 5cm (2 in) of aquatic compost.

14 Place a dwarf lily, (*Nymphaea pygmaea*) carefully in the basket on top of the compost so that the top of the root ball is about 3.75cm (1½ in) below the top of the basket. Add compost around the plant, but do not put any on the top of the root ball, which should protrude about 2.5cm (1 in) above the soil.

15 You need to cover the top of the compost with gravel to hold it in place and prevent it from floating to the surface when you add the water. Slowly and gently tip the gravel on top of the compost, levelling it out with your hands. You do not need much gravel, just enough to cover the surface. Trim any excess hessian from the sides of the basket with scissors.

16 Use a scrap piece of hessian to polish the tiles and give them a real shine. Then put a 10-cm (4-in) layer of gravel on the bottom of the pot. Carefully position the lily basket on this or, if necessary, add height with a few bricks so that the lily floats on the water surface. You can add other plants, such as a double marsh marigold and an iris, which would need brick supports to raise them to the correct height.

FILLING YOUR WATER FEATURE

Decide where you want to position your water feature and move it into place before you fill it with water because it will be heavy and difficult to move once it is full. When filling the pot, put the hose at the bottom and turn the tap on gently so as not to disturb the compost and gravel in the plants too much. When filling or cleaning the water feature, allow the water to overflow from the top of the pot. This will flush through any debris and prevent the water from becoming stagnant.

A HOMEMADE HAMMOCK

What could be more idyllic than relaxing in a hammock on a hot summer's afternoon, with a good book and a long, cool drink? With this hammock, you can enjoy all this and feel virtuous, as you have done all the hard work!

TOOLS

6-mm (¼-in) drill bit

Countersink bit

Scissors

Tape measure

Power drill/ Screwdriver

Hammer

Pencil

Tenon saw

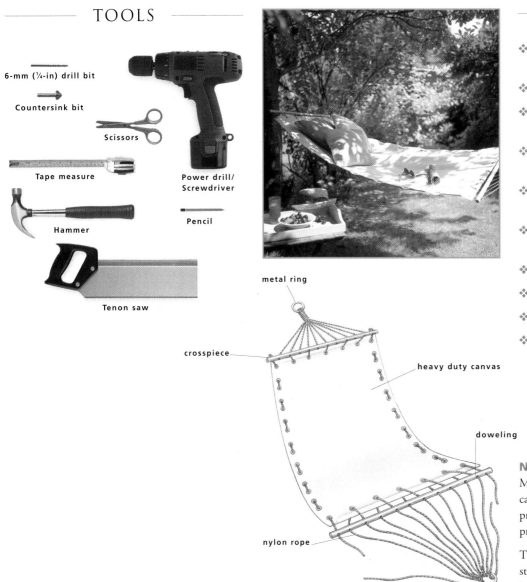

metal ring

crosspiece

heavy duty canvas

doweling

nylon rope

MATERIALS

❖ Heavy-duty canvas 90 by 200cm (36 by 80 in)

❖ Double-sided carpet tape, 5cm (2 in) wide

❖ Doweling, 1.25cm (½ in) in diameter, 1.5m (5 ft) long

❖ Doweling, 2.5cm (1 in) in diameter, 1.8m (6 ft) long

❖ 1-cm (⅜-in) brass eyelets, including the tap and die

❖ Nylon rope, ½cm (³⁄₁₆ in) thick, 20m (63 ft) long

❖ Two metal rings, 5cm (2 in) diameter

❖ Two metal cleats

❖ Sandpaper

❖ Set square (optional)

NOTES

Most arts and crafts shops and haberdashers sell canvas. Buy the heaviest weight available. If you prefer, you can use deckchair canvas, which will provide a dramatic splash of colour.

The nylon cord used for this project has a breaking strain of 90kg (200lbs) and all materials are of the best quality. However, we do not recommend that the hammock be used by more than one person of average weight at any one time.

STARTING OUT – STEPS 1 TO 4

1 If your canvas is not cut to size, spread it out on a flat surface and mark a rectangle measuring 90 by 200cm (36 by 80 in). Use a straight length of wood or a long ruler to draw the lines. Cut along the lines with a pair of scissors.

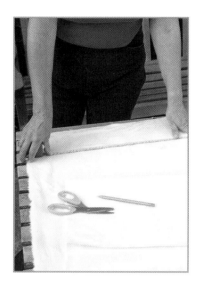

2 Draw a line parallel to, and 5cm (2 in) from, each edge of the canvas. Then draw a line 10cm (4 in) in from each side. These guidelines show you where to stick the double-sided carpet tape. Make sure that all the corners are squared up – you may need to use a set square to help you.

3 Starting at one end of the hammock, firmly stick the double-sided tape to the canvas between the two lines you have just drawn. The guidelines will help you keep the double-sided tape straight. When pressing the tape onto the canvas, take care that it does not crease or buckle.

4 Measure and cut out two lengths of 70cm (28 in) on the 1.25-cm (½-in) diameter doweling. Keeping the canvas and tape as flat as possible, carefully peel off the backing paper on the double-sided tape on the two short sides. You may need someone to help you keep the canvas flat because the double-sided tape is very sticky.

SIZING YOUR HAMMOCK

You can make a hammock any size you wish. The size given here is for an average height. If you are below average height, or if you are making the hammock for a child, you can make the hammock shorter. A short person on a long hammock means that it will sink lower than usual in the middle. To make a hammock that is an appropriate length for your personal use, add 90cm (3 ft) to your own height – this measurement will be the length of canvas you need to buy. Then follow the rest of the steps to make the hammock.

PUTTING IT TOGETHER – STEPS 5 TO 8

5 Rub the ends of the doweling that you cut in Step 4 with sandpaper to eliminate any splinters. On the short side of the canvas, position one of the dowels on the tape against its outside edge, and press it down firmly.

6 Fold the canvas over the dowel so that the edge of the canvas aligns with the far edge of the tape and the guidelines you drew earlier. Press the canvas down firmly onto the tape, taking care not to crease or buckle it. Repeat Steps 5 and 6 for the other short side of the canvas.

7 To avoid bulky corners when you fold the canvas over, cut out a small square, measuring about 5cm (2 in), from the corners of the hammock.

8 Now peel off the backing strip on one of the long sides and fold the canvas over so that the canvas edge aligns with the guideline drawn in Step 2. Work your way slowly down the side of the canvas, pressing the tape firmly in place. Repeat for the other long side.

CARPET TAPE

Carpet tape is essentially a very strong double-sided tape and is used here in place of a sewn hem. (A sewn hem on a thick canvas would require an industrial sewing machine!) The advantage is that the fabric is bonded into a double thickness, preventing fraying at the edges, and making a stronger bed to fix eyelets into. The tape itself does not support the weight, but because it is originally intended to hold carpet down, it can be relied upon to last as long as the canvas does (see Notes on page 48).

PUTTING IT TOGETHER – STEPS 9 TO 12

9 At each short end of the hammock, mark the centre points of the seven eyelets. Place a tape measure across the end inside the ridge made by the covered dowel and make a mark at 2.5, 15, 27.5, 40, 52.5, 65 and 77.5cm (1, 6, 11, 16, 21, 26 and 31 in) from one end. Mark these same measurements at the other short end.

10 Place the canvas on a hard surface, such as a small paving slab. Using the tap and die provided in the eyelet kit, place the die directly under the first pencil mark. Push the tap onto the canvas so that it fits snugly into the die underneath. Hit the tap sharply with a hammer, cutting a neat circle in the canvas.

11 Cut all the remaining holes in the same way, then put in the eyelets. The eyelets come in two parts. Place the part with the flange in the die and push this up through the hole in the canvas. Put the other part of the eyelet over the flange and hold it in place with the tap. Hit the tap sharply with a hammer to join the two parts together. Repeat for the other eyelets.

12 There are also decorative eyelets in the long sides of the hammock. Mark their positions 2.5cm (1 in) from the edge of the folded canvas. From one end, measure and mark the centre points of the holes at 20, 25, 42.5, 47.5, 65, 70, 87.5, 92.5, 110, 115, 132.5, 137.5, 155 and 160cm (8, 10, 17, 19, 26, 28, 35, 37, 44, 46, 53, 55, 62 and 64 in). Cut the holes at these points as before and then insert the eyelets.

ALL ABOUT EYELETS

Eyelets are obtainable from ships' chandlers (yachting suppliers) and are used to strengthen holes in canvas sails and nylon tarpaulins. They are sold complete with assembly tools and instructions and come in a range of sizes. Most eyelets are brass, but plastic versions are also on the market. They seal the raw edges of the fabric and spread the strain, which is their function on the shorter ends of the hammock. However, besides being practical, they also look very decorative and they are used in this way on the long edges.

PUTTING IT TOGETHER – STEPS 13 TO 16

13 To make the crosspieces, measure and mark two 80-cm (32-in) lengths of 2.5-cm (1-in) diameter doweling. Support the doweling so that the waste wood overhangs the edge of your workbench, and cut out the lengths.

14 Smooth the sawn edge with a piece of sandpaper. Then, using a long ruler or a straight piece of wood as a guide, draw a line along the length of each dowel.

15 Make a mark 2cm (⅞ in) in from one end and then mark every 7cm (2¾ in) along the line – you should have a total of 12 marks along the line. Make sure that the dowel is positioned firmly, then drill holes at each of these points using a 6-mm (¼-in) drill bit.

16 Do the same for the second piece of doweling. Then countersink each hole on both dowels. Sand each piece smooth with sandpaper.

SAFETY TIPS FOR DRILLING HOLES IN DOWELING

When drilling holes in doweling or any circular piece of wood, take extra care that the wood doesn't slip. Use a vice or g-clamp to hold the wood securely – if the drill slips, your doweling will be ruined. However, if you are an experienced woodworker and are fairly confident using a power drill, you can wedge the doweling into the gaps on a workbench or table, as shown above. But always use a bradawl or nail to break the surface of the wood before you start drilling. Begin slowly, then speed up.

PUTTING IT TOGETHER – STEPS 17 TO 20

17 You are now ready to start threading the rope through the hammock. The easiest way to do this is to place one end of the hammock near to, and parallel with, the edge of the work table. Hold it in place by hammering a nail through the first eyelet on either side. Measure the midpoint and position the bottom of one of the metal rings 30cm (12 in) up from this point. Hold the ring in place with a nail.

18 For each end of the hammock, you will need 7.2m (24 ft) of rope. Wind some adhesive tape around the ends of the rope to make it easier to thread. Thread most of the rope through the ring, leaving about 30cm (12 in) outside the ring. Thread the rope through the second hole in the dowel and the second eyelet. Thread the rope through the third hole in the dowel, and back through the ring, leaving about 30cm (12 in) slack.

19 Continue threading the rope in this way, leaving the last hole in the hammock and dowel free. Check that the tension of the rope is even in each length, then return the taped end of rope through the ring. Take the other end and double it over to form a loop (see also the diagram on page 110).

20 Hold the loop and the slack lengths of rope and start winding, or whipping, the untaped length of rope around this loop. Pull the rope tight each time. You need to whip it around the loop at least ten times.

PROFESSIONAL TIP

When binding the end of the nylon cord with insulating tape, add an extra twist to make a pointed end which will make threading a whole lot easier. It is important to keep all the lengths evenly matched, as this will stop the hammock from twisting and ensure that the weight is evenly distributed along the length of the canvas. Whipping needs practice: try out your technique before working on the hammock. When the tension is right, the effect is very neat and the you will be able to easily pull the loose end up inside the coil.

PUTTING IT TOGETHER – STEPS 21 TO 24

21 After you have whipped the rope, thread it through the back of the remaining loop, while keeping the other length taut. Pull on the rope so that the loop closes around the taped length of rope to form a knot.

22 Holding the whipping firmly, pull the untaped length of rope so that the knot is pulled halfway inside the whipping. Cut both ends of the rope as close as possible to the whipping. Repeat Steps 17 – 22 for the other end.

23 Cut two 2.25-m (90-in) lengths of rope for the sides. Wrap tape around the ends as before, and thread the rope through the last hole in the dowel. Pull it through and tie a knot at the untaped end. Weave the rope in and out of the eyelets until you reach the dowel at the other end. Thread the rope through the dowel and secure with a knot. Cut off any excess rope.

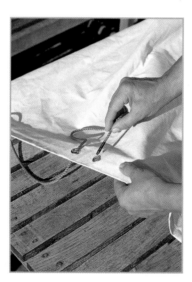

24 Thread the rope along the other side in the same way, knotting the end of the rope after threading it through the dowel. Finally, attach a cleat to each of the rings. Your hammock is now ready for hanging from secure fixings (see below).

WHERE TO HANG YOUR HAMMOCK

The wonderful relaxation of lying in a hammock comes from being suspended and in motion – rocking gently from side to side. The height from the ground is immaterial, but to be on the safe side, we suggest lower rather than higher, especially if young children are likely to clamber into the hammock. Supports obviously need to be sturdy. Choose two strong tree trunks, if you are fortunate enough to have two suitably spaced ones in your garden, or a wall bracket and a tree, or a free-standing hammock support.

A STEPPED PAVED PATH

An informal stepped path makes a charming link between the upper and lower levels of this garden. The emphasis is on the natural look, with rounded beach pebbles and chestnut stakes setting off simulated terracotta concrete slabs.

TOOLS

Sledgehammer Shovel

Brush

Garden spade

Float

Garden sieve

Tenon saw

Rubber mallet

Bucket

Lump hammer

Bricklaying trowel

Bolster chisel

Garden trowel

Spirit level

MATERIALS

To make two steps, each one measuring 90 by 107.5cm (36 by 43 in):

❖ Forty chestnut wood stakes, 50cm (20 in) long

❖ Twenty concrete paving slabs, about 24 by 24cm (9½ by 9½ in)

❖ Beach pebbles, about 5kg (11 lbs)

❖ Length of wood batten, the width of the path or longer (see Step 2)

❖ One bucketful garden soil (see Step 3)

❖ One 25-kg (55-lb) bag of ballast

❖ One 25-kg (55-lb) bag of cement

❖ One 25-kg (55-lb) bag of soft sand

❖ Two 25-kg (55-lb) bags of sharp sand

❖ Dishwashing detergent

❖ 14 bricks

❖ Thyme seeds

VARIATION

❖ Sand

❖ Small potted plants, such as herbs

❖ Old paving slabs

NOTE

In this project two paved steps are made. If two such steps suffice, the work can easily be done in a day. If you want to make a longer run of steps, you must allow a correspondingly longer amount of time in which to complete the work.

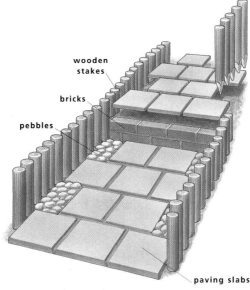

wooden stakes

bricks

pebbles

paving slabs

STARTING OUT ~ STEPS 1 TO 4

1 Clear the pathway of the old paving as well as any large stones or plants. Next, line both edges of the path with wooden stakes. Push the pointed end of the stake into the ground and hammer it down halfway with a sledgehammer. Hammer the next stake flush against the first, and continue adjusting the depth until the tops make a gentle curve running down the slope of your pathway.

2 To determine the exact width of the path (three slabs wide in this case), lay three concrete slabs on a flat, hard surface. Place some beach pebbles on either side and then measure this width. Cut a piece of wood batten to this width. Now hammer in a parallel row of stakes using the length of wood to measure the distance between the two lines of stakes. Each time you hammer in another stake, use the wood to check its position.

3 You will need to dig foundations for the front of each step to give them extra support. Using your garden spade, mark a line in the soil between the stakes, 90cm (36 in) from the top of the slope. Dig a trench along this line, the width and depth of the spade. Save a bucketful of the soil you remove to use later and distribute the rest in a suitable part of the garden.

4 Next, mix some concrete. On a hard surface make a mound of ten shovelfuls of ballast. Sprinkle two shovelfuls of cement on top. Mix the two together by pushing your shovel into the mound and lifting and turning the ballast and cement mixture over. Continue mixing until it is a uniform colour throughout.

WOODEN STAKES

Wooden stakes were chosen to act as a natural barrier alongside the path in order to make a gentle, visually pleasing transition between the hard surface of the path itself and the flower beds running alongside it. The stakes have a dual role, being both functional and decorative. Not only do they provide a strong and effective barrier to keep the soil off the path, but with the passage of time and exposure to the weather, they will mellow and look even better as nearby foliage drifts over them.

PUTTING IT TOGETHER - STEPS 5 TO 8

5 Make a cavity in the centre of the mound and half fill it with water. (Don't add too much, you need to make a fairly stiff consistency.) Work your way around the mound, pushing the mixture into the water. Continue until you have a stiff mix of concrete.

6 Scoop the concrete into a bucket with your shovel and pour it into the trench you dug in Step 3. Because it is a stiff mixture, you will need to shake the bucket to help it come out. The concrete should cover the bottom of the trench evenly and be level with the top of the downward slope. Using a float, smooth the surface of the concrete. You may need to add more concrete to the trench to level it off.

7 Then, make some mortar by mixing five parts of soft sand with one part cement (see below). Use a bricklaying trowel to lay a bed of mortar on top of the concrete.

8 Lay the short edge of the brick, or header, close to the wooden stakes. Put some mortar on the header of another brick, and lay this next to the first, pushing the two together. Lay the next brick in the same way. If you need to cut a brick in half, position a bolster chisel about halfway along the top of the brick and hit the chisel with a lump hammer. Repeat this on the other sides until the brick breaks.

PROFESSIONAL TIP

Add a squirt of liquid detergent, such as dishwashing liquid, to the water before mixing your mortar. The detergent softens the water and makes it easier to work with. In addition to this, it also helps make the mortar more plastic and keeps it from "going off" or hardening too quickly, which sometimes can result in cracking. It is useful to have a mortar that remains workable for a longer period because it allows you time to work at a slower pace, and this is likely to give a neater result.

PUTTING IT TOGETHER - STEPS 9 TO 12

9 Lay a bed of mortar on top of the first row, or course, of bricks. Position the first brick of the second course so that it straddles the join between two bricks below. Continue laying the second course. Use the trowel to gently tap the bricks down into position each time.

10 Now make sure that the soil of the first step is level. Push the tip of the spade into the soil and drag it gently backward and forward, smoothing the surface so that it is slightly below the top of the bricks. You may need to add or remove soil to achieve a flat surface.

11 Next, mix a coarser mortar using five parts sharp sand and one part cement. Add enough water to the mix so that it just falls off the trowel. Scoop the mortar into a bucket and pour it over the levelled-out soil. Using the tops of the bricks as your guide, push the mixture around the step with the float to create an even bed of mortar, about 2.5cm (1 in) deep.

12 To make sure water can drain away, the mortar needs to slope down slightly from the top of the step. Take a spirit level and place one end on the bricks and the other on the mortar towards the back of the step. The mortar should be slightly higher at the back. Add or remove mortar to achieve this.

PROFESSIONAL TIP

Use a stiff mixture of concrete when laying the foundations, as this will allow you to lay the bricks directly on top, enabling you to complete the project in a day. Don't forget, though, that the mortar and concrete will need time to set. Do not walk on your completed path for at least 24 hours, otherwise you could misalign the slabs and have a uneven path. You may like to add an individual touch such as the date or your initials (or both!), which can be done quite simply by pressing pebbles into the wet concrete.

PUTTING IT TOGETHER - STEPS 13 TO 16

13 Temporarily position the paving slabs by laying them lightly on the bed of mortar. Make sure that the first row overlaps the bricks by 5cm (2 in), and that they are spaced evenly. Using the first row as a guide, position the next row of slabs so that each slab is behind a join in the first row. Continue until you have positioned all the slabs.

14 When you are happy with their positions, carefully lift each slab off the mortar. You will find that the slabs leave an indentation in the mortar and you can use this as your positioning guide.

15 Place some mortar for the first slab on the step, making sure it covers the top of the brick course. Position the first slab firmly on top of its indentation in the bed of mortar, remembering that it needs to overhang the bricks. Then, take a rubber mallet and gently tap the surface of the slab so that it is secure in the mortar. Put down more mortar and lay the rest of the row in the same way.

16 As you lay the second row of slabs, make sure that you keep a slight downward slope. Lay your spirit level on the slabs and use the rubber mallet to tap down the slabs where necessary, to maintain this slope. Continue laying the slabs for the next two rows and check the slope of each row with the spirit level.

PROFESSIONAL TIP

It is vital that both the slabs and the bricks have an equal resistance to frosty conditions. If one crumbles, it will spoil the whole appearance of the path. Before you buy them, make sure you check with your supplier that the bricks and slabs are suitable for outdoor use and all weather conditions. Modern concrete slabs are cast in faithful reproductions of all manner of natural stones. The moulding and tinting is so convincing that it is hard to tell the difference from the real thing.

PUTTING IT TOGETHER – STEPS 17 TO 20

17 Now that the slabs are in place the areas at the side of each row and the end can be filled with beach pebbles. Take a handful of pebbles and drop them into the mortar. Push them gently into place. As the mortar sets, it will hold the pebbles securely.

18 Being careful not to tread on the first step, make the second step in the same way. Remember to use your spirit level to check that this step also slopes slightly to allow water to drain away.

19 By the time you have completed the two steps, the mortar in the brickwork will have had a chance to dry. You can now remove any excess from the joins. Take a stick, and, being careful not to gouge too deeply, gently drag it along the horizontal join, leaving about 1.25cm (½ in) at each end. Repeat for the other joins. Then, fill in any gaps where the slabs overlap the bricks.

20 Now prepare the bucketful of soil you saved in Step 3. Remove all the stones and break up any big lumps of soil by passing it through a garden sieve.

GIVING A PATH AN IDENTITY

This path is laid without the need to cut any of the paving slabs to size, and the variation of this project (on page 64) uses old broken paving stones. However, any irregular shapes that arise during the laying can be filled with beach pebbles, which not only look attractive but also help water drain off the steps. Don't worry about trying to match the arrangement of paving slabs between steps. The eccentric nature of the arrangement of the slabs on each step gives the path an individual identity and adds to its rustic charm.

FINISHING IT OFF – STEPS 21 TO 24

21 Using the garden trowel as your measure, mix together eight scoops of soil and four scoops of sharp sand (see below).

22 Spread out this mixture with your trowel, and sprinkle some thyme seeds evenly over the top. Use the trowel to mix the seeds and the soil together.

23 Next, sprinkle the soil mixture over the joins of the slabs with the trowel. Use a brush to push the mixture into the joins between the slabs. Tap it down with the brush making sure that it is tightly compacted into each join.

24 When all the joins have been filled, brush the mixture onto the next step. With the brush, push the soil mixture into the joins as before. When you have filled all the joins, sweep the remaining soil away. Take care not to get any of the soil around the beach pebbles.

A SWEET-SMELLING PATHWAY

Sieved soil and sharp sand are mixed at a ratio of two to one – two measures of soil to one of sharp sand. This improves the drainage properties of the soil and prevents it from becoming a solid lump in the rain. Thyme seeds are added to this mixture, which is then used to fill the gaps between the slabs. The advantage of the low-growing thyme plant is that it not only breaks up the the shape of the slabs, but as the thyme grows, it will release its subtle perfume, creating an attractive and fragrant pathway.

VARIATION - USING BROKEN SLABS

1 For a different look, you may want to reuse old or chipped paving slabs for your path. Lay down an even thickness of sand, packing it down tightly. Position the irregular-shaped slabs along the length of the path. Use the spirit level and a rubber mallet to make sure they are level. In between these slabs place bricks on their sides, banging them into position, level with the surrounding slabs.

2 Fill other gaps in the path with smaller slabs. Line both sides of the path with beach pebbles, pushing them down hard into the bed of sand.

3 Mix together some sharp sand, soil and thyme seeds as in Steps 21 and 22 on page 62. Brush this mixture into the gaps between the slabs and bricks. Use the brush to tap the mixture down into the gaps.

4 Small plants, such as potted herbs, provide a useful and attractive finishing touch. Plant these in the larger gaps, near to the sides of the path.

FINDING INSPIRATION

Keep your eyes peeled for unusual or attractive paths when browsing through gardening or style magazines, visiting gardens or looking at gardening books. Make notes and sketches, or take photographs. These sources will help you come up with something really individual when you create your own path. Be on the lookout for suitable materials in garden centres. If you see a tile, slate or slab that appeals to you, buy just one. Take it home and see how it looks before committing yourself to a truckload!

SEASIDE SANDBOX

Bring the seaside to your garden with this boat-shaped sandbox. A lid keeps the elements and inquisitive animals out, and there is provision for a parasol to be hoisted above the seat in very hot, sunny weather.

TOOLS

Pencil

Filler knife

3-cm (1¼-in) flat drill bit

Electric sander

16-mm (⅝-in) flat drill bit

Countersink bit

3-mm (⅛-in) drill bit

Power drill/ Screwdriver

G-clamp

Jigsaw

Tape measure

Crosscut saw

Mitre saw or block

Combination square

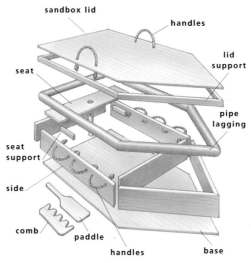

sandbox lid

handles

seat

lid support

seat support

pipe lagging

side

comb

paddle

handles

base

MATERIALS

❖ Two 1.8- by 1.2-m (6-by 4-ft) sheets of plywood, 1cm (⅜ in) thick

❖ 6m (20 ft) of planed wood 15 by 2.5cm (6 by 1 in)

❖ Four 1.8-m (6-ft) lengths of planed wood, 3 by 2cm (1⅛ by ¾ in)

❖ Four 1.8-m (6-ft) lengths of sawn treated wood, 5 by 2.5cm (2 by 1 in)

❖ No. 6 cross-head screws, 2.5, 3 and 3.75cm (1, 1¼ and 1½ in) long

❖ Plastic pipe 3cm (1¼ in) diameter, 25cm (10 in) long

❖ Foam pipe lagging, 3.75cm (1½ in) in diameter, 4.5m (15 ft) long

❖ Quick-drying wood-coloured filler

❖ Sandpaper

❖ Water-based wood stain, assorted colours

❖ Wood adhesive

❖ Nylon rope 16mm (⅝ in) in diameter, 3.6m (12 ft) long

❖ Silver sand

VARIATION

❖ Large pieces of scrap plywood

❖ Sandpaper

❖ Water-based wood stain

STARTING OUT – STEPS 1 TO 4

1 Mark a rectangle 90 by 165cm (36 by 66 in) on one of the sheets of plywood. On each of the longer sides, measure and mark 45cm (18 in) from one end. Measure and mark 45cm (18 in), the midpoint, on the shorter edge. Then, using a long ruler or length of wood, draw a diagonal line from the midpoint to the marks on each side, to complete the "bow" of the boat-shaped base.

2 Raise and support the plywood above the ground using blocks of wood or flat stones. The plywood should be at least 10cm (4 in) above the ground, so that the jigsaw blade can cut freely. Position the jigsaw blade on the waste side of the wood, and cut out the shape. You may have to reposition the supports as you cut.

3 To make the sides of the box, measure and mark two 85-cm (34-in) lengths and two 120-cm (48-in) lengths on the 15- by 2.5-cm (6- by 1-in) plank. Draw a line across the wood at these marks, using your combination square to keep the lines straight. Hold the wood firmly on a suitable support and cut out each length with a jigsaw.

4 On each end of the longer lengths draw a line 1.25cm (½ in) in from and parallel to the end. Along each of the lines mark three evenly spaced points. Drill a pilot hole at each mark, then countersink each one. Hold one of these lengths at right angles to one of the shorter pieces and fix them together with 3.75-cm (1½-in) screws. Do the same to the other end. Now turn the structure over and screw the remaining length of wood into position.

SAFETY FIRST

Before using any power tools, always familiarise yourself with how they work. Make sure that the power cord is kept safely away from the working parts, and for additional safety, use a circuit-breaker in case you accidentally cut through the cord. Practice new or difficult cuts on a piece of scrap wood and only work on the real pieces when you are confident of your ability. If you are not sure about using a particular tool, seek professional advice from an expert or ask someone who knows how to use it to help you.

PUTTING IT TOGETHER – STEPS 5 TO 8

5 Place the four sides on the base and draw a line along each of the inner edges: this marks the width of the sides on the base. Now place the base on top of the sides, leaving the end triangle overhanging. Drill and countersink a hole in each corner, then screw each corner to the base using 3.75-cm (1½-in) screws. Continue drilling pilot holes and adding screws at roughly 10-cm (4-in) intervals.

6 To make sides for the triangle of the base, set the blade of the jigsaw to a 45° angle and cut the end of a piece of 15- by 2.5-cm (6- by 1-in) wood. Place this cut end on one of the corners of the box and make a mark that corresponds with the apex of the triangle. Draw a line at this mark with a combination square, then make another 45° cut along this line. Do the same for the other side of the triangle.

7 Drill and countersink two pilot holes at each end of one of the sides and at only one end of the other (you only need one set of screws at the apex). Position the sides on the base and screw them into the sides of the rectangular box with 3.75-cm (1½-in) screws. Then screw the apex together. Turn the sandbox over and screw through the base into the two sides, using 3.75-cm (1½-in) screws and spacing them at 10-cm (4-in) intervals.

8 To make the seat, measure the inside width of the box at the back of the boat shape. In this case, the measurement is 90cm (36 in), but for accuracy, you should always measure your own. Cut a length of 15-cm by 2.5-cm (6- by 1-in) wood to this length.

YOUR WORK SURFACE

An object as large as this will need to be made outside – a flat, paved patio area would be most suitable. You need a dry, flat, hard and level surface with an electric point nearby for power tools. Use wooden planks to raise the wood above the paving so that the wood can be drilled through without damaging the ends of the drill bits. If you have a portable workbench, use it to secure lengths of timber as you drill or saw. If not, a sturdy stool or box and a set of G-clamps will do.

PUTTING IT TOGETHER – STEPS 9 TO 12

9 To make the seat supports, measure and mark 20cm (8 in) on a length of 3- by 2-cm (1⅛- by ¾-in) wood. Use a combination square to draw a diagonal line at 45° to this mark, so that the longest side of the wood to be cut is 20cm (8 in). Cut along this line with a jigsaw. Cut out another 20-cm (8-in) length in the same way.

10 Drill and countersink two holes 3.75cm (1½ in) from each end of the seat support. To position the supports on the inside of the box, measure and mark a line 10cm (4 in) up from the base on each side of the box. Position the top of the seat support on this line, so that the mitred edge is facing downwards. Holding the support firmly, screw it into place with 3-cm (1¼-in) screws.

11 For the parasol support, measure and mark the midpoint on one of the long sides of the seat, then measure 5cm (2 in) up from this point. Hold the seat securely and drill a hole at this point using a 3-cm (1¼-in) flat drill bit (see below).

12 Draw a line 20cm (8 in) in from the back of the sandbox. Position the seat along this line, place the flat drill bit vertically in the hole and push it down so its point makes a mark on the base. Take the seat away, raise the base on a piece of wood, then drill a hole through the base.

PROFESSIONAL TIP

Flat or spade drill bits fit into any power drill and enable you to make large neat holes for doweling or other round shapes. The bit's end is flattened to the diameter of the hole with a sharp central point for precision location. They come in a range of sizes. Use a bradawl to make a hole first and place the bit's point in it, then hold the drill absolutely vertical and proceed as usual to drill the hole. No more than usual pressure is needed, but it is vital to keep the drill at 90° to the wood, or the parasol will slope off at an angle.

PUTTING IT TOGETHER – STEPS 13 TO 16

13 To secure the seat, drill and countersink two pilot holes 17cm (7¼ in) and 10.5cm (4¼ in) from each end and 3cm (1⅜ in) down from the top of the sandbox. (Check that these holes are just above the seat support.) Place the seat on the supports, so that the front edge aligns with the top of the diagonal of each support. When in position, fix into place with 3.75-cm (1½-in) screws.

14 Place a length of 5- by 2.5-cm (2- by 1-in) wood on each long side of the base to reinforce it. Make sure the ends are aligned, then secure them with 3.75-cm (1½-in) screws, making sure that you screw into the sides of the box and not through the base. Secure two more lengths on the base, making sure they are evenly spaced and long enough to run to the front of the boat.

15 Using the side of the sandbox to guide the jigsaw, cut off the waste lengths of battens. Take extra care when doing this to cut as close as possible to the side of the boat without cutting into it.

16 To make the holes for the rope handles, turn the sandbox on its side and draw a line 5.5cm (2¼ in) down from the top edge. On this line, mark the six holes at 25, 47.5, 55, 77.5, 85 and 107.5cm (10, 19, 22, 31, 34 and 43 in) from the end of the sandbox. Use a 16-mm (⅝-in) flat drill bit and remember to clamp a piece of wood under each hole before drilling to prevent the wood from splitting. Repeat for the other side.

PROTECTING THE UNDERSIDE

Adding battens to the underside of the sandbox serves two important purposes. Sand and children are both heavy, and the battens help to strengthen the base, making it less likely to sag or buckle under their weight. In addition to this the battens serve to lift the sandbox off the ground. This prevents the underside of the sandbox from resting on wet ground, allows air circulation and lessens the likelihood of rot. Use treated wood battens, as these will also deter wood-eating bugs and beetles.

PUTTING IT TOGETHER - STEPS 17 TO 20

17 To make a support for the parasol, push the plastic pipe into the hole in the seat and down into the hole in the base. Mark with a pencil where the pipe meets the top of the seat. Pull the pipe out of the hole and cut along this line with the jigsaw. Push the pipe back into the seat – it should be flush with, or just below the seat. For safety's sake, make sure that there are no sharp edges on the plastic pipe.

18 You need to position the pipe lagging temporarily so that you can accurately measure the size of the lid. To cut the lagging, insert a utility knife into the top of the indented line that runs along the length of the lagging. Pull the knife slowly towards you to slit open the lagging.

19 Cut mitres in the lagging to make neat corners. Place the lagging at the appropriate point in a mitre saw, making sure that the slit you have cut is at the bottom. Hold the lagging steady and slowly cut a mitre at the end.

20 Starting from the triangular point of the sandbox, pull the lagging apart along the slit and slide it onto one long side. When you reach the middle cross-section, use the utility knife to cut out a square to allow the lagging to fit over the cross-section.

SOFTENING THE EDGES

Although it was not designed with this particular use in mind, foam pipe lagging really does provide a protective edging that is second to none. Its shape fits the timber well, it is easy to cut and it is not only soft, but resilient and weatherproof too. Some children will always be bumping and scraping themselves, but by fitting this barrier you will certainly prevent at least a few of the minor accidents that inevitably arise in moments of high excitement. It also, incidentally, looks in keeping with the boat shape.

PUTTING IT TOGETHER – STEPS 21 TO 24

21 The lid of the sandbox overhangs slightly, so it will be slightly larger than the base. Lay the second sheet of plywood on a flat surface and place the sandbox upside-down on top of it. Trace around the sandbox holding a length of 3- by 2-cm) (1⅜- by ¾-in) wood between the sandbox and your pencil. Then cut out the lid with a jigsaw.

22 Now, using the lid as your guide, measure and cut out five lengths of 3- by 2-cm (1⅜- by ¾-in) wood to go along each underside of the lid. Drill and countersink holes on these lengths of wood at regular intervals. Cut a mitre where ends meet, or alternatively, you can leave a small gap. Secure the lengths of wood to the lid with 2.5-cm (1-in) screws.

23 Drill holes for the rope handles on each side of the sandbox lid, using the 16-mm (⅝-in) flat drill bit. Position the holes 5cm (2 in) from each side and 67.5cm (27 in) and 90cm (36 in) in from the back. Remove the pipe lagging from the sandbox and cover all the screws with filler. When this has dried, sand the whole box smooth, rounding off all the sharp edges.

24 Paint or stain the sandbox with a quick-drying, water-based wood stain or paint in bright colours on different parts of the sandbox. When the stain is dry, apply some wood adhesive to the tops of the sides of the box and press the pipe lagging onto it. To make the handles, thread rope through holes in the lid and in the sandbox and knot the ends.

CHOOSING SAND

When filling your sandbox, the best and most economical way to buy sand is from a builder's yard or from a garden centre. Ask for silver sand – which is a dry, white and very fine type of sand – and avoid the cheaper builder's sand recognizable by its brighter yellow colour. While this will not harm children, it does stain clothing. A sandbox needs to be quite full to give the right kind of "beach" feel, so buy an extra bag if you are in doubt. Always cover the sandbox when it is not in use because it will attract cats from miles around!

VARIATION – COMBS AND PADDLES

1 Draw the outline of three paddles on a piece of scrap plywood. Make a template and trace the shapes, or draw them onto the plywood freehand. Hold the plywood firmly and use the jigsaw to cut these shapes out.

2 Make another template to draw the simple comb shape. Cut this out from plywood, as before. You can make the teeth of the comb pointed in the template if you wish – when you cut out the shape, you can cut off the points.

3 When the shapes have been cut out, sand them down smooth, making sure that all the edges are rounded off.

4 Finally, using a quick-drying water-based wood stain, paint each of the toys a bright colour. You may need to apply several coats to achieve the desired effect, but remember to leave each coat to dry before starting the next.

MAKING TOYS

Playing in sand does not require elaborate equipment and clues as to what is appropriate will come from observing your own child at play. If roadways are the choice, simple bulldozer pushes can be made; a wooden comb can simulate a ploughed field and a paddle shape can be used to flatten the surface. Combs and paddles are simple shapes for which you can make your own templates. A broomstick can be cut up and used to sink holes, and wooden or thick-cardboard boxes make good moulds for building walls.

FINISHING IT OFF – STEPS 21 TO 24

21 Check that the table top fits by slotting it in position. Use a spirit level to make sure that it is flat – a prerequisite for any table surface!

22 To prolong the life of your table and also to make it more attractive, paint or varnish it. You will need to dismantle the table again before painting the various parts. Make sure you have a clean paintbrush, as well as a few rags on hand to mop up any spills. If you wish to protect the surface you are working on, cover the ground with old newspaper or a dust sheet.

23 Paint the bench seats in a coloured wood-stain. (See page 79.) Wood stains are supposed to be translucent so that you can see the grain of the wood through them. However, you can build up the intensity of the colour by applying more layers of paint, without losing the effect. Make sure each coat of paint is completely dry before applying another layer.

24 Contrasting colours look very effective on the table. However, you can pick any colour scheme that suits your garden. Finally, add a coat of clear varnish over the finished paint to further protect the table against the weather.

FURTHER PROTECTION

The corners of the side panels are the only part of this table that touch the ground. If you want to protect them from damp ground, cut a strip of roofing felt to the right length and tack it into place with panel pins. Alternatively, you can buy furniture feet from most hardware stores. Screw two of these on each side to lift the table off the ground. The disadvantage of these is that they can make the table wobble, so take extra care when positioning the table to make sure that it is on flat ground.

1

I
P
(
one of
on the
bricks
side, ar
(½ in) a
a gap c
each br

3

washed
not ha
large sl
your sh
heap o
two sh
the two
over fr
with yo
unifor

The
sand
muc
con

PUTTING IT TOGETHER – STEPS 5 TO 8

5 Starting at one end, lay a trowelful of mortar on the ground between the chalk lines drawn in Step 2. Drag the trowel back through the mortar, wiggling it from side to side, to create a trough in the middle. (This will help the bonding of the bricks and ensures an even thickness of mortar.) Avoid laying mortar over the chalk line.

6 You are now ready to lay your first brick. Position it in the corner of the back row and push it down into the bed of mortar. Make sure it is in the middle of the chalk lines. When it is in place, tap it down firmly with your trowel.

7 Take another brick and apply mortar to the header (short) face. Push the tip of your trowel into the middle of the mortar to make an indentation. This helps the two bricks bond together.

8 Taking care not to let the mortar fall off the end, push this brick against the first brick and down into the mortar. Remember to keep it in the middle of the chalk lines on either side. Lift away any excess mortar squeezed from the joints as the bricks are pushed together (see below).

PROFESSIONAL TIP

Each time you spread mortar on the bricks, you will find that some drops off onto the ground. You will step in it if it is not cleared up, and spread it around the work area in no time at all! Get into the habit of picking up any loose mortar and scraping away the mortar that oozes out between the bricks as you are adding them. This can be lifted on the trowel and returned to the bucket or board to be re-used. Keep an old dustpan and brush specially for outdoor work and use them to sweep away specks and splashes.

PUTTING IT TOGETHER - STEPS 9 TO 12

9 When you have completed the course of bricks at the back, check that they are level. It is important to establish a level from the start and to continue checking each course. Also, check that they are in line by holding the spirit level in front of the bricks. Tap with the trowel where necessary to correct their position.

10 When laying the side bricks, make sure that they are at right angles to the back. Use a combination square to check this angle. Tap the brick into place with your trowel and make sure it is secure in the mortar.

11 Lay the second course of bricks so that each brick is above a joint in the course below. This means that you need a half brick at each end. To cut a brick, lay it on a hard surface and position a bolster chisel halfway across its stretcher (long) face. Hit the chisel with a lump hammer. Turn the brick to another side and repeat until it breaks in half.

12 Be careful not to knock the brickwork as the barbecue walls grow taller. It will be unstable for about 24 hours, until the mortar has set. When laying the corner bricks, use the handle of your trowel to tap them into place, remembering to lift off any excess mortar with your trowel as you go.

BREAKING BRICKS

If you have the right equipment, bricks can be cut in half with surprising ease. A bolster chisel is a strong, broad-bladed instrument with a short, thick handle, and a lump hammer is a rubber-headed mallet that spreads the force of a blow along the full width of the chisel blade. Score or mark the brick with the chisel where you want to make the cut. Put the brick on a flat surface and the hold the chisel blade on the cutting line, with the handle slightly tilted. Hit the chisel with the lump hammer and the brick will break cleanly in two.

PUTTING IT TOGETHER – STEPS 13 TO 16

13 Check that each course of bricks you lay is level. Place the spirit level vertically against the end, back and sides of the brickwork, and tap the bricks gently into place. You should also check the interior width of your barbecue with your tape measure each time. Continue for six courses.

14 Lay the barbecue hearth on top of the sixth course of bricks to check its size. The slate for the hearth needs to completely cover the bricks at the back and sides (see below).

15 Lay a bed of mortar on top of the sixth course of bricks. With someone helping you, position the slate so that its front edge lines up with the front of each side wall. Once you have it in position, push it into the bed of mortar. Remove any excess mortar, then lay another course of mortar and bricks on top of the slate, in line with the courses below.

16 On the eighth course of bricks, you need to make ledges for the grill shelf by positioning two bricks on each side at right angles to the course. Lay the back row first, then position the first brick of a side wall so that a quarter of it overhangs the course at each side. Tap it into place with your trowel. Lay the next brick as usual, then finish the course with another ledge brick placed at a right angle.

PROFESSIONAL TIP

If you find it difficult to get hold of a large slab of slate that you can have cut to the desired size for your barbecue, a suitable alternative would be to use a large paving slab. The principal feature of whatever material you choose is that it should be able to resist heat and has to be able to hold the hot, burning coals without shattering or cracking. Slate and paving slabs are heat resistant and are especially well-suited because they can be hosed down for easy cleaning.

PUTTING IT TOGETHER – STEPS 17 TO 20

17 On the ninth course of bricks, lay two ledge bricks on each side of the barbecue and also one at the back. Make sure that the ledge bricks on the side are not directly over those in the course below. You will need to cut some bricks so that the courses are of equal length. On the final course of bricks, place one ledge brick on each side, above the ledge bricks on the eighth course, closest to the back.

18 To work out where to position the extra wall, lay the wooden decking on the ground, with one edge hard up against the side of the barbecue. Draw a chalk line at the opposite side of the decking. If you want an extra wall and decking shelf on both sides of the barbecue, repeat this on the other side.

19 The extra wall should be nine courses high, the same height as top of the first ledge brick on the barbecue. Because of the thickness of the slate, the top course needs to be thinner than the others. Using the technique in Step 11, you will have to cut the bricks *lengthwise* in the ninth course. Attach a length of string to the first course at the front of the barbecue, and use this to align the first brick of the extra wall.

20 Once the barbecue and the extra wall have been built, the mortar will be dry enough for you to tidy up the joints. Take a stick and gently drag it along the horizontal joints between the courses of bricks to make an indentation. Repeat for all the other joints, but be careful not to put any pressure on the walls. Finally, brush the walls and surrounding area clean.

USING GUIDES

Before adding mortar, lay out a single course of bricks in the shape of your barbecue, allowing spaces for mortar between the bricks. Draw a chalk line to mark this position. This will help you to keep in line and make sure that both sides are of equal length for the first brick course. A length of string pulled taut between two bricks on a hard surface can be used to check the alignment of the two extending walls. Taut string forms a natural straight line that is easy to follow.

FINISHING IT OFF – STEPS 21 TO 24

21 The warming shelf (see diagram on page 86) should be narrower than the grill shelf, so that it won't get in the way of what's cooking underneath. Measure one of the grill shelves and mark the required depth. Hold the shelf firmly on some bricks or on a workbench and cut it with a hacksaw. Smooth the cut ends with wire wool, then rest the shelf on the top two ledge bricks.

22 Slot the grill shelf into position so that it is resting on the four lower ledge bricks. It should sit securely on these ledges, giving you a stable surface on which to cook.

23 Rest the decking work surface on top of the wall and the corresponding ledge on the side of the barbecue. Remember that this is not securely fixed, so do take care when using the surface.

24 With a bradawl make three holes on the front edge of the decking. Screw a cup hook into each hole. You can hang your cooking utensils from these, so that they are within easy reach.

BARBECUING SAFELY

Build the fire toward the back two thirds of the slab so that there is no danger of hot embers falling out. Use proper long-handled barbecue tools to keep your arms clear of the heat. Keep a bucket of water nearby to damp down the fire if it becomes too hot. The coals should be left to burn for about half an hour before cooking begins, to give a more gentle, even heat that is less likely to cause fat to spit and flames to flare up. A wood fire is less predictable. As a precaution, keep a first aid kit to hand while barbecuing.

TREE-TOP BIRDHOUSE

A birdhouse not only encourages birds into your garden, it also provides them with shelter when nesting. Make sure that the entry hole is not too large, or predators and larger birds may be able to get in and disturb a nesting pair.

TOOLS

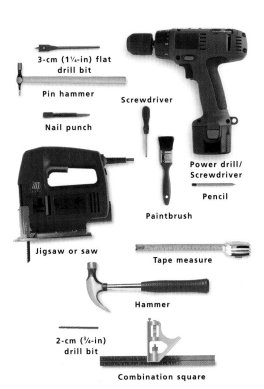

3-cm (1¼-in) flat drill bit

Pin hammer

Nail punch

Screwdriver

Power drill/ Screwdriver

Pencil

Paintbrush

Jigsaw or saw

Tape measure

Hammer

2-cm (¾-in) drill bit

Combination square

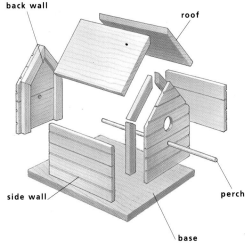

back wall

roof

side wall

perch

base

MATERIALS

❖ Two 1.8-m (6-ft) lengths Dutch Profile tongue-and-groove boarding

❖ Exterior wood adhesive

❖ Wood batten, 2- by 2-cm (¾- by ¾-in), 90cm (36 in) long

❖ Panel pins, 2cm (¾ in) long

❖ Sandpaper

❖ One 30- by 120-cm (12- by 48-in) pine shelf, 2cm (¾ in) thick

❖ Nails, 3 and 5cm (1¼ and 2 in) long

❖ Doweling, 30cm (12 in) long, 3.75cm (½ in) in diameter

❖ Quick-drying exterior matt varnish

❖ Hook and chain

VARIATION

❖ Sandpaper

❖ Emulsion paint, grey and off-white

❖ Piece of 15- by 2.5-cm (6- by 1-in) pine shelf, 70cm (28 in) long

❖ 3-mm (⅛-in) drill bit and No. 8 non-corrosive screws

❖ Weatherproof wood filler

❖ One 1.8-m (6-ft) length 5- by 5-cm (2- by 2-in) sawn treated wood (see Note)

NOTE

If you make the variation, the end of the 1.8-m (6-ft) length of wood will be buried in the ground – so make sure you treat it with a suitable preservative.

STARTING OUT – STEPS 1 TO 4

1 Start by marking the lengths for the sides on a piece of Dutch Profile tongue-and-groove. You need to measure, mark and cut out four 25-cm (10-in) lengths. You may find it easier to measure one length, then mark and cut this before marking the next ones, or you may prefer to mark them all and then cut them all together.

2 Next, mark lengths for the ends of your birdhouse. Measure six 21-cm (8½-in) lengths of tongue-and-groove. Take care when measuring so that the pieces are all the same size and will fit together neatly.

3 Cut the tongue-and-groove along the lines you have drawn. If you are using a jigsaw, make sure that the lead is long enough to allow you freedom of movement.

4 To make the end pieces, apply a wavy line of wood adhesive in the groove of one of the 21-cm (8½-in) lengths and slot the tongue of another into it. Add two more lengths in the same way, so that one end is made up of three pieces. Make the other end with the three remaining lengths. To make each of the side walls, glue two 25-cm (10-in) pieces together in the same way. Leave the glue to dry.

LOCKABLE TAPE MEASURES

A lockable tape measure is an essential item, and enables you to measure and mark a length of wood on your own, since both hands are free. This kind of tape measure also has a mechanism to recall the end back into the casing. Most tape measures are calibrated in both imperial and metric measurements, which means there is less chance of making mistakes in any conversions. Always stick to one set of measurements, either imperial or metric, throughout any one project.

PUTTING IT TOGETHER - STEPS 5 TO 8

5 When the glue has dried, mark and cut out the roof point on the two end pieces. To do this, first measure and mark the midpoint on one of the shorter sides. Then, you can either draw lines down to the sides at a 45° angle using a combination square, or measure 10cm (4 in) down from the top on each side, and draw a line between the points and the midpoint. Cut out the roof point with a jigsaw or saw.

6 Measure the height of the sides of the end pieces. This is the length of the short side before the peak you have just cut. It should measure about 15cm (6 in), but it is best to measure your own to be accurate. Compare this measurement to the height of the side pieces and trim them to fit, if necessary.

7 Working on the inside of one of the end pieces, hold an offcut of tongue-and-groove on its side along the edge of the end piece, then place a piece of batten right up against this. Draw a line along the edge of the batten. This shows you where to glue the batten. Repeat on the opposite side and on the other end piece. Trace two more batten widths along the roof sides, but do not use the tongue-and-groove width here.

8 Cut the batten to the required lengths. You need to mitre the ends slightly so that all the roof supports will sit together snugly. Apply a wavy line of wood adhesive inside your guideline on one of the ends of the birdhouse. Place the batten in position close to your pencil mark so that the tongue-and-groove will fit alongside it. Repeat for the other three sides and the other end piece.

USING WOOD GLUE TO JOIN SURFACES

It is a mistake to think that the more glue you use, the better the adhesion you will achieve – this is simply not the case. In fact, wood glue contains water and as it dries the water evaporates. If you have used too thick a layer of glue, gaps will appear at this stage. So be sparing with your glue. In order to get the best results, apply an even, thin coating of glue to both surfaces to be joined. Then rub them together to create a suction between the two surfaces that encourages the bonding.

PUTTING IT TOGETHER - STEPS 9 TO 12

9 For extra strength, nail panel pins into the batten from the right side (the outside of the birdhouse). You will need about three pins for each side and two for each side of the roof, spaced evenly along the edges. Nail punch the panel pins so that their heads lie below the surface of the wood.

10 Mark the entry hole for the birds on one of the end panels. This should be centrally located about 12.5cm (5 in) from the bottom. Place the marked piece on a block of wood or on a workbench, and drill the hole using the 3-cm (1¼-in) drill bit. Mark and drill a 1.25-cm (½-in) hole for the perch about 7.5cm (3 in) from the bottom. Sand inside both holes (see below).

11 You are now ready to assemble your birdhouse. Apply a line of wood adhesive along the edge of one of the end pieces and fit it against a side panel. Hold in place for a minute or so until the adhesive "takes". Repeat on the other end and leave the glue to dry.

12 Now measure, mark and cut out the roof from the pine shelf. One piece needs to be 21 by 30cm (8¼ by 12 in) and the other slightly smaller at 19 by 30cm (7½ by 12 in). The remainder of the pine shelf will form the base of your birdhouse.

PROFESSIONAL TIP

It can be awkward sanding inside the holes, especially if you do not have fingers that are long and thin! You may find it easier to find a piece of wood with roughly the same diameter as that of the hole. Wrap a piece of sandpaper around this and work it through the hole. A pencil is about the right diameter for the perch hole. For larger holes, use a length of doweling. Try to smooth the wood as much as possible so that the perch can be glued snugly into the hole. Pre-drilled holes only need slight sanding with fine sandpaper.

FINISHING IT OFF – STEPS 13 TO 16

13 Place the slightly smaller piece of roof on one of its longer sides, and apply a line of wood adhesive along the other edge. Glue the slightly larger roof piece to this so that the edges butt together. Hold for a few minutes while the glue "takes", then hammer about three evenly spaced 5-cm (2-in) nails along the edge.

14 Position the roof on top of the birdhouse. Using your eyes as a guide, make sure there is an even distance at the front and back and glue into position. When the glue is dry, hammer nails into the supporting battens. Nail punch the nails so that their heads lie below the surface of the wood.

15 To make the base, measure the bird house and add about 5cm (2 in) to the length and width: cut out a piece of pine shelf this size. Centre the house on the base and draw around it. Using a scrap of tongue-and-groove as a guide, mark where the batten goes along the inside of the side panels of the birdhouse. Cut two lengths of batten to fit and nail them into place.

16 Push a length of doweling through the small hole to make the perch. On the back, measure 7.5cm (3 in) up from the bottom of the birdhouse and hammer a nail through to hold the perch in position. Paint your birdhouse with wood stain or varnish. When the paint has dried, place the house over the base and secure with glue and nails. Screw a hook into the middle of the roof to hang the birdhouse from a chain.

CENTRING OBJECTS ON A BASE

The easiest way of centring a square or rectangular object is to position it close to one edge of the base (say on the length of the base) on which you are working and measure the excess on the other side. Divide this measurement in half and draw a line at this point. Then position the object on another edge (on the width) and, once again, measure the excess. Halve this and draw a line at this point. Position one corner of your object at the point where the lines cross and you will find that it is centred on the base.

VARIATION - FREESTANDING BIRDHOUSE

1 Make the birdhouse following Steps 1 to 16, but do not secure it to the base. After sanding the birdhouse and its base, paint both sides of the base. Turn the birdhouse upside down and paint under the eaves of the roof with grey emulsion. Turn it up the right way and paint the perch, finishing with the top of the roof.

2 When this paint is dry, paint each side of the house with off-white emulsion (see below), making sure you paint carefully around the base of the perch. When the paint is dry, secure the base to the birdhouse with glue and nails.

3 Copy the shape on page 110 onto the 15- by 2.5-cm (6- by 1-in) wood, making each square 2.5cm (1 in). Alternatively, you can design your own shaped bracket. Use the jigsaw to cut out four brackets, then sand each bracket smooth. Drill and countersink a hole in each of the vertical and horizontal arms of the brackets.

4 Position a bracket in the middle of the post so that its top is flush with the end and screw it into place. Fill the holes with filler, then paint the support. When the paint is dry, secure the birdhouse on the brackets by screwing up through the pilot holes in the horizontal arms of each support. Bury the end of the post about 45cm (18 in) into the ground, or you can make extra supports to stand it up above the ground.

PAINTING THE BIRDHOUSE

An interior-quality paint is used to paint the birdhouse because, after exposure to the elements, it will show signs of weathering more quickly than an exterior paint. This will give the birdhouse a rustic look in a relatively short span of time. If you are not keen on a "weathered" birdhouse, use an exterior paint or wood stain. If the colour you want is only available in emulsion, use it, but cover it with two or more coats of an exterior-quality varnish after the paint has dried.

PUTTING IT TOGETHER – STEPS 5 TO 8

5 Keep the mix in a mound and make a cavity in the middle. Add a little water to the cavity, push the top of the mix into the water, then continue to turn and mix in water. Add more water if necessary, but remember that it should be a stiff mix of concrete (see tip box on page 103).

6 Scoop the concrete into a bucket and sprinkle it evenly along the bottom of the trench. It needs to cover to a depth of at least 10cm (4 in).

7 Use the float to spread the concrete around the trench. Hold the float on the surface of the concrete, patting and smoothing it down. You will probably need to compact the concrete down, as it will be quite stiff.

8 Now make some mortar. Use five parts of soft sand to one part cement and turn the mix with your shovel until it is a uniform colour. Add enough water so that the mortar just falls off your shovel. Working on one side at a time, load the bricklaying trowel with mortar, then let it slide off onto the trench foundations. Drag the trowel through the bed of mortar, moving it from side to side to create a jagged surface.

DRYING TIME FOR FOUNDATIONS

This is one project where we advise you to cheat a bit and spread your "day" over two weekends. The strongest foundations will be achieved by a slow drying process, so ideally you should split this project into two parts. The foundation concrete can be laid and covered with a plastic sheet until the actual brick laying is done some days later. Some settling will occur as the concrete dries and this could affect the wall's stability, so aim to get the foundations solid – and you will be making a garden feature to last a lifetime.

PUTTING IT TOGETHER - STEPS 9 TO 12

9 Starting at one corner, lay the first brick on the bed of mortar, pushing it down firmly. Add a layer of mortar to the header (short) face of the next brick. Push the tip of the trowel into the mortar to create an indentation, which helps the bricks bond. Butt the end with mortar on it against the laid brick, pushing it firmly into the bed of mortar.

10 Use a combination square to help you make the corners straight, using the handle of the trowel to tap the bricks into place. To lay the next layer, or course, place mortar on the laid bricks, then lay each brick of the next course over a joint in the course underneath (see box below).

11 On the fourth course of bricks, the first above ground level, you need to create weep holes (see tip box on page 106). This course is laid as before, except that you do not need to put mortar on the header faces of the middle brick on each of the sides of the herb bed. Remember to leave a gap at these joints – do not push the bricks hard up against each other.

12 To check that a wall is level, use a spirit level. Place it on top of the course of bricks and use the handle of your trowel to tap the bricks at the relevant points to maintain the horizontal level of the bricks.

PROFESSIONAL TIP

Bricklayers make building a wall look like child's play, but the rhythm of their work has built up over the years. As a novice, you will need to work slowly and carefully to achieve a neat result. Lay the first brick in the bed of mortar, then "butter" the end of the next one and butt it up against the first. Tap the end with the trowel handle and lay the next one. When you add the next course, the mortar will squeeze out below. Scrape it off with the trowel and return it to the rest of the mortar. Keep checking the wall with a spirit level.

PUTTING IT TOGETHER – STEPS 13 TO 16

13 On the fifth course, leave gaps on each side of the herb bed through which plants can grow. To do this, lay a corner brick, then leave a gap the size of one brick. Then lay another brick, pushing it into position and cleaning off any excess mortar with your trowel.

14 These large gaps are decorated with "tile creasings" (see diagram on page 102). The tiles need to be about 5 by 10cm (2 by 4 in), with at least one straight edge. If you are unable to get tiles this size, you can break your own. Take a larger tile in your hand and use the edge of your trowel to break it up until you get the size required.

15 In the middle of the gap in the brickwork, lay some mortar, then lay the tile pieces, keeping the straight edge showing. Lay enough tiles to bring them level with the top of the bricks (about three tiles). Continue laying bricks, creating a gap on each of the sides and putting in the tiles.

16 On the next course, add a gap on each side, as before, but position the gaps so they are not directly above one another. Check that the walls are vertical with a spirit level. Use the handle of the trowel to tap it into a vertical position, making sure the walls are straight. Continue until you have six courses of bricks above the ground.

CREATING WEEP HOLES

Weep holes help water drain out of the herb bed. They are easily created by omitting mortar from the cross joints in the first course of bricks above ground. Without weep holes, the soil will easily become waterlogged, and whatever plants you have planted in your herb bed are sure to suffer. In a herb bed of the size used here, you need to have about six weep holes. If your herb bed is larger or smaller than the one made here, you will have to allow for more or fewer weep holes.

PUTTING IT TOGETHER - STEPS 17 TO 20

17 The final two courses of bricks are laid using a technique called corbelling. This is where the bricks overhang the course below. Lay a bed of mortar on the bricks, then a course of bricks as normal, except that the stretcher (longer) face should overhang the course below by about 2.5cm (1 in). Position the first and last brick so that its side and end overlap the corner. Tap into place and remove any excess mortar.

18 You will find, because of the overhang, you need a little more brick. Cut a brick to the required length by placing the bolster chisel on top and hitting it hard with the lump hammer until it breaks off. This piece can then be used to finish the course of corbel. Finish off by laying another course of corbel.

19 Leave the mortar to firm for about 30 minutes, then tidy up the joints. Hold the trowel diagonally on the mortar in a joint. Press down firmly and run it along the joint creating a diagonal face on the mortar. Repeat this in all the vertical and horizontal joints.

20 Use the pointing trowel to clear the excess mortar out of the weep holes. Brush the walls to remove any excess mortar. Now leave the mortar to set overnight before filling the bed with soil and planting the herbs.

VARYING THE CORBELLING

An imaginative approach to the corbelling on the herb bed can turn it into an even more strikingly decorative feature. Think of introducing different colour bricks into the corbel, perhaps in alternation with the basic colour or for the whole run. The mellow grey-yellow of old bricks could be contrasted with a dark brown brick, for example. Alternatively, old glazed bricks will add an eye catching, luminous note to the structure, especially if the glaze has crackled with age.

PUTTING IT TOGETHER – STEPS 21 TO 24

21 Put a 5-cm (2-in) layer of gravel across the bottom of the herb bed. Then start to fill the box up with peat-free compost until you are level with the openings in the brickwork. Take a small plant and push it into one of the openings, packing compost around it from the inside, so that it is firmly embedded in the gap.

22 Take a large piece of tile and place it against the back of the plant in the gap. Pack compost around this to hold it in place. The tile will stop the compost spilling out of the gaps.

23 Place pieces of tile behind the tile creasings, then pack compost behind them to hold them in place. You can also push beach pebbles into the gaps in the same way. Alternate between the tiles, pebbles and plants on different courses of bricks.

24 When you have filled in all the gaps, finish filling the box with compost or loam. Plant the remaining herbs in the top of the bed.

CHOOSING PLANTS

Select herbs that enjoy a free-draining soil such as the Mediterranean herbs: scented rosemary, thyme, marjoram and oregano. A small bay tree, chives, fennel and tarragon will give even more variety and culinary choice. Mint must be grown in a pot to limit the spread of its roots. The gaps can be filled with creeping varieties of thyme, alpine strawberries and helianthemums (rock roses), which will add colour to the display even though they are not strictly herbs. You could also consider underplanting with bulbs for a spring display.

APPENDIX

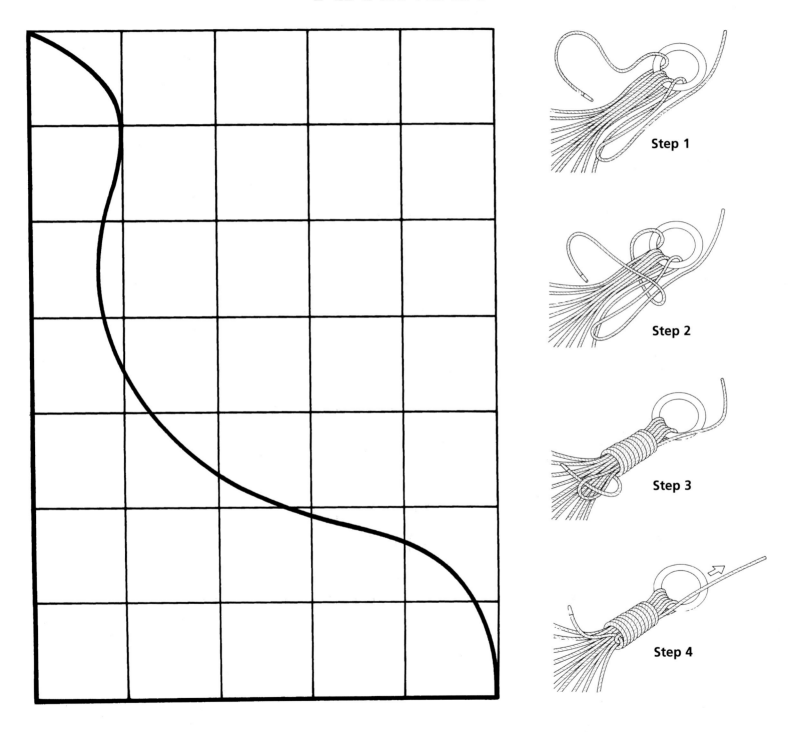

Step 1

Step 2

Step 3

Step 4

INDEX

GARDEN PROJECTS: *Acknowledgements*

The author would like to thank and acknowledge the hard work of the following people:

Sally Walton for being my wife; **Stephanie Donaldson** for styling and allowing us into her home; **Jack Howell** and **Paul Roberts** for their craftsmanship; and **Steve Differ** for always being there with a helping hand.

Marshall Editions would also like to thank **Joanna Stawartz** and **Philip Letsu** for design assistance; **Belinda Weber** for editorial assistance; and a special thank you to **Emile** and **Felix McKenna**.